A Nameless Wrestler

A

NAMELESS WRESTLER.

BY

JOSEPHINE W. BATES,

AUTHOR OF "A BLIND LEAD," ETC.

———

PHILADELPHIA:
J. B. LIPPINCOTT COMPANY.
1889.

Copyright, 1889, by J. B. LIPPINCOTT COMPANY.

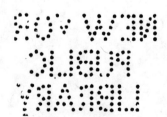

A NAMELESS WRESTLER.

CHAPTER I

AFAR in the North-west, cutting its tortuous way through the barrier of the Cascades, flows the Columbia River. A regal stream it is, of rugged ancestry. The mountains rise in towering ridges, pushing their white crests through the outer veil of clouds and piercing into the very sanctuary of the sky; against the blue their wrinkled summits rest as though they belonged not to the earth, but to the vast outer world beyond. Down their giant slopes the sable clouds roll sullenly, but they heed it not; the fitful temper of the cloud is not of them. The wild currents of the gale sweep up, rioting about their heads and ploughing the snow into monster furrows on their brows, but they heed it not; the restless spirit of the storm is not of them.

Bleak, beautiful domes! Cold, aspirant peaks! The white of the crest drops softly into gray; faintly the gray grows ribbed with radiating streaks of dun; then the brown ledges of denuded rock are standing out bare and bald; the lighter tints are deepening, the dun, the bronze, the shading green,—they have darkened into the long stretches of the mighty forests.

3

That vast, unbroken, undulating sea of forest! On it rolls, on and on, and only the surging waves of that other vaster sea beating against the cliffs can call the limits of its empire. A reach of primal wilderness! A rich undese-crated glory of growth! Through the dense leafage the bright sun slants and glimmers feebly, but in the matted tangles of the undergrowth it is held suspended, for the net-work of tall brush, intertwined with tough fibres of the vine-maple, makes a very jungle under whose woven canopy at mid-day there is twilight. Places there are, a plenty, into whose deep recesses the fitful gleam of a broken ray, even, has never pierced; haunts where the bear and the cougar rally, but the sun cannot find his unaccustomed way. Ferns in a tropic exuberance of growth lift their tall stems above the mossy hollows, and fir needles falling through centuries have spread a carpet fragrant and soft as down.

No desolation of boles, stark and spectral in the winter woods, of gaunt, snow-shrouded skeletons, shade our revery to wistful discontent. Summer and winter is hung the same rich tapestry; summer and winter alike maintain the dusky splendor of the forests.

And, oh, the wonder of the waters! Those myriad cas-cades whose voice enshrined in the name of the range shall proclaim their beauty forever! Their song is never silent; their music never dies away. Down from the frozen heights they come, pure and clear; vaulting the crags, leaping the precipices, and plunging along the mystery of the woods; singing in ever-varying cadence, gathering, swelling, till the glad notes break at last into the thunderous pean of the river. It sings the triumph of labor; for its course lies through cañons, through gaps and gorges, between precipitous walls that beetle aloft among the clouds. It has chiselled its rocky path; in the patient persistence of ages it has burst its slender rift, forced its widening wedge, and grown by mastery to the power with which at last it sweeps its waters onward resistlessly to the sea.

In its victorious stretch of open sway it is joined by the Willamette, coming down from the matchless fields of sunny Oregon. A soft-voiced Sybarite this, diverting itself with many an amorous advance to grassy slopes, and many a sly embrace of blooming islands by the way. No urgent toil through mountain barriers; but soft lapsing of banks that melt into yellowing fields, an easeful course along the luxury of the valley.

A little distance from its mouth, where an island has set its bar to the river's further commerce, is a city, Portland. In site and surroundings the place is generously favored. To the back a terrace of hills cuts off the prospect, but elsewhere the view is unbroken. In front, winding with languorous grace, flows the stream, on whose opposite bank lies the eastern segment of the town. Beyond is a belt of open valley; then, like rounded billows of the ocean, the foothills roll back, larger, ever larger, till away in the distant mountains they seem breaking against the sky.

The dull green of the nearer vegetation, flecked with amber or brown as a field of grain or a clearing intervenes, creeps with a darkling shade across the rising swells, and climbing the forest ridges in sombre mood throws itself against the far horizon, and lies a broken line of black against the blue.

Standing out in vivid isolation, mute herald's of earth's throes, blind sentinels of the ages, four snow-capped peaks tower imperially. Gaunt, assertive Hood, of broken slopes and arbitrary lines, intolerant of analysis, disdainful of curves, leaves to Adams his massiveness and frontal failure, to St. Helen's her arched impersonal grace; for in his own rough ruggedness of strength he finds a nobler bearing.

Yet Hood is not the patriarch of the peaks; for over the shoulder of St. Helen's, dim and hazy in the distance, is the serrated crest of Tacoma, a hundred and fifty miles away. Viewing its faint, far summit, the mind projects that sublimest of landscapes, the white Olympian range overlooking the peaceful waters of the perfect Sound, and this grim, glacier-ribbed picket keeping his eternal guard at the farthest outpost of the nation.

The town of Portland, though now so prosperous and reasonably proud of its position, was in 185– what by contrast could claim to be scarcely more than a collection of shanties set down in the wilderness. Later, when the mining excitement of the Salmon River and the Boise Basin made of Portland a supply-dépôt, it acquired the character of a commercial centre, and its growth was very rapid. But before, it was simply the village of an outlying farming district; and farther back yet, the nucleus of the village had been itself a farm. A few far-sighted pioneers had drifted in, entered the land, and settled upon it. The soil was very rich, and others soon followed, in the gregarious instinct of the race locating near at hand. So the country grew, and with it Portland.

During the early period of the settlement, when as yet only in concept lay the destinies of the town, among the simple farmers came a man who was not one of them. Where Martin Fennimore had passed his life,—for he was old; where he had made his money,—for, contrary to the general condition, he had some: these were questions no one asked and no one knew. The stranger's aspect did not invite familiarity, and the diffidence of his neighbors held them from a trespass upon his reserve.

A Norwegian owned a claim adjoining the site; Martin Fennimore bought it and took possession. Soon, by dint of his growing influence, he got the land incorporated with the town, and commenced selling lots and growing rich. Then, whether prompted to it in a season of unaccountableness (for the old man was believed to have such), or anticipating the future in a fuller faith, he erected a house whose like would be to-day conceded a thing of pretensions, but which was then amid the surroundings of the wilderness truly palatial.

The occupancy of the grand house confirmed the man's position. He was the foremost citizen of the place, rose by natural assent to the highest public office, and then in the panoply of his dignities he retired again quietly to private life.

It was the year before the first great mining excitement.

Portland had not yet begun her stride forward in the strong impetus to come with the army of men pressing forward to the gold fields. Still, there was a general atmosphere of tension and expectancy. Some prospectors had gone in already to forestall the rush, and money was finding its way from the quiet little town to the larger promise of the diggings.

It was whispered that Martin Fennimore's snug little pile had been withdrawn from the bank and invested in a quartz lead, which report served to strengthen the common credit in the find. But this was only gossip; no one could trace the assertion to an authority. Meanwhile, the conservative majority awaited fuller information, and in dearth of assurance held to the safety of its rural interests.

CHAPTER II.

In the lingering glow of the sunset, stealing out through the twilight of the trees that encircled Martin Fennimore's grand house, might be seen the figure of a young girl. She kept close within the shade, creeping warily, and pausing at intervals to scan the wide-arched windows; and the survey seemed reassuring, for, unlatching softly the small rear gate, she glided through it to the open path that led into the woods.

She dropped her air of caution now, and advanced carelessly, slipping off her hat in playful challenge to the wind, whose flagrant liberties she took with a smile that became her mightily. She was light of foot and light of heart, this fresh, young thing, and in her sauntering she struck occasionally into a soft snatch of song, breaking it off abruptly to mock the chattering squirrel, or to mimic the drowsy lark that was settling into her nest. The active, insistent life about touched, in her, electric fibres; the bright-tinted flowers that grew beside the road she stooped and plucked with delight, for she was in harmony with nature, but only in its happy, sensuous aspects. She had no sight for the grand old trees, or the expanding depths of the sky; she felt no thrill of awakening thought, or joy of contemplation.

Yet the trees were worth a glance, as they reared their

huge, branchless trunks aloft, and broke suddenly into such arch of limb, such profusion of darkling foliage, that the bright sunset trickling through was like jewels pendulous from the boughs. Overhead, following the trend of the path, was a narrow vista of sky. Off to the north it shone a dull sapphire, across which passed the pale opal trail of a cloud. The nearer heavens wore a feverish glow; but the sun crept lower, the flush floated slowly across the narrow pass and was hidden in the mazes of the forest. The wood with its pensive shades, the sky with its waning lights, both were lost upon the young girl, for she was akin only to the brightness.

Yet it was not that nature had failed to endow her with a full capacity, that she seized the sensuous in a dearth of faculty for anything beyond. No coarse, irresponsive spirit was ally to a form of such modelling,—a form attuned in every line to shaded harmonies and subtle touch. Indeed, an artist would say the slender figure was of too delicate a grace for ideal beauty. One suspected that the soul would be a sensitive, nervously-organized thing, unfit for much in the rough-and-tumble scrimmage of life. Yet when by chance the girl raised her head, and one caught the gleam of eyes large, dark, and glowing, he felt his thoughts confounded under her straight, strong gaze. An unlooked-for element had entered in,—forest and fire in ominous union. The pliant figure, the translucent skin, the wavering curve of the lip,—these were much; but those vagrant lights, changeful, wilful,—were they not more?

What product in character shall be the resultant of such forces? which shall prevail, the weakness or the strength? which shall guide, circumstances or the native energy of the soul? and of what quality that energy shall prove,—these are problems that admit no prediction, but such natures are born, alas! to tumult.

One felt an undefined portent of a time when those bright flowers might lose their charm, and the silent depths of the forest grow suddenly companionable; when that free, untroubled spirit, being smote upon, might vibrate henceforth strongest to the low, base chords of nature and experience. But the future gathers its clouds to its own bosom; to-night not a shadow rested upon the sunny head save that which fell protectingly from the shelter of the dim fir woods.

She was evidently no debtor to time, for she stepped out of the path to gather some ferns and some moss that was clinging about the roots of an old stump. Then, sauntering along again, she emerged at last on the shelving slope of the river bank.

She glanced hastily up and down the clearing, but no one was in sight; so, withdrawing a little into the woods, she seated herself upon a fallen tree-trunk and proceeded to assort her flowers. She had scarcely settled to the work when a man stepped lightly over the log from behind, and seated himself beside her.

"I wish you would make your appearance more gradually, Allan," she said, with pretty petulance. "There is such a suggestion of coyotes about these moving shadows that I am always startled at your abrupt way of presenting yourself."

"Coyotes!" he said, with a smile at the childishness; "they never make appointments."

"But they might be rude enough to intrude upon one."

He laughed, a man's amused laugh at a girl's timidity. Perhaps it was in an instinct of protection that he passed his arm about her; perhaps it was in the sense of added security that she allowed it to remain.

"If I shall have no rival more formidable than these thievish marauders, I shall hold myself lucky," he asserted. "The carnivorous is not what daunts me in love."

"It didn't seem to me that anything daunted you," she said, archly.

Her tone was not very severe; one surmised that the young man's passion was not a very grave offence in his lady's eyes. Indeed, it might appear that she rather favored his aspirations, she was so placidly tolerant of his love-making. She even permitted him to take without protest the blossoms from her belt, though it seemed to necessitate an added pressure of the encircling arm to accomplish it. But when, in addition, he stooped and slyly kissed her, she straightened up and shook her head in the perverse temper of infantile tyranny.

"Forgive me!" he said, with mock repentance.

"Well—well—if it was an accident—yes."

"It was an accident, certainly."

But she drew away, notwithstanding, to a polite distance.

"It is liable to be a little unsafe off there," he expostulated;

"those moving shadows, now, look surprisingly alive. In case of attack you will want to be nearer shelter."

"It isn't the carnivorous that daunts me in love," she echoed, maliciously.

"Come!" he offered, in truce. "I will not transgress again. Besides, I want to report progress. I hung the brackets for the potted plants yesterday, and this evening I devoted to the ivy. It has grown till now it encircles the whole archway in the dining-room."

"It is very pretty, I am sure." She was drawing near again. "We must have another just like it on the other side, that the whole door-way may be green. I hope you trained the ivy high, and made the curve graceful; there is nothing that affronts the eye like an awkward, carelessly-trained vine."

He smiled, in spite of himself, at the lurking criticism of what she had not seen.

"Probably I haven't got it quite as an artist would, but a few of your touches will set it right,—if you will ever arrange to transfer yourself to its vicinity," he added, in a tone whose banter betrayed an undercurrent of earnestness.

"I am coming, Allan, of course." She was irritated at the conditional. "Furthermore, I'm coming soon, but—young gentlemen mustn't show impatience; it isn't in taste."

He glanced into her face, with its little, imperious pout, and sighed. Her seventeen years had left her still a child, and his twenty-two had made him a mature man. That she could attribute to impatience his anxiety, showed how little she was

2

capable of realizing the difficulty and the delicacy of his po
sition. But he could not pay for her appreciation the price
of her innocence, or sow the germs of unrest by a discussion
of his man's fears and perplexities. He could not tell her
that Martin Fennimore's opposition to their union was an
ever-present dread, and his own poverty a nightmare. She
was a creature of such unreliable attributes, at once so vacillating and so tenacious, that he felt always insecure when he
ventured a reference to anything that was debatable. Just
now, as his remark seemed to have jarred upon her mood,
he cloaked his wistfulness and, entering into her own light
vein, said, carelessly,—

"Whenever you wish, dear. The house is ready, and I
shall go on twining vines about it till you come; but I warn
you that henceforth I shall train them all awry, so that your
conscience for art, if nothing else, had better hasten your
decision."

"In other words, you entreat a concession at the point of
the sword. What an adroit diplomatist! And what a docile
lover! Well, I don't know but I approve of stratagem—
when it succeeds; and this is clever enough to deserve success. You want more dexterous fingers, do you, to shape
your curves? Mine are almost too pretty for service,"—she
held them up for her own innocent admiration,—"still, you
have a sort of lien, I suppose, upon my hand, and—and—
you may recall your threat. Lo! I rescue the vines."

She put the soft fingers into his palm and left them there
in capricious abandonment.

"Jean!" he cried, clasping the hand with suppressed energy, "do not trifle. Love may be an incident to you; it is life to me." His voice was unsteady; its earnestness was infectious, and the coquetry vanished from her smile.

"I suppose I am wrong not to feel more," she said, reflectively. "But someway I can't get so sober and solemn over our engagement as you do. I should be content to just drift along: these stolen interviews are so delightful!"

"You are a child, Jean. We cannot just drift along; we must be married."

"Yes, I suppose we must; you always say so. Besides, I have promised."

"Promised! Do you not love me?"

"Oh, yes; I love you, of course."

The avowal had such girlish dispassionate candor that he shivered. She knew as much about love as a lisping infant; no more. But he had no right, he reflected, to expect her to love with his man's ardor; intensity was not possible to souls of such pure distilling.

"Jean," he said, with a half-sigh, "you keep a fellow perpetually distracted. You allow appointments, you make confessions, you promise marriage, and yet I can pin you to nothing. Come, don't you think you are a little despotic? don't you believe you ought to redeem your promise?"

She looked away. Something in her lover's reproach stirred the zeal of her young loyalty. She was studying, and intently, for the arched brows were drawn, and her eyes were taking slowly that strong, direct light which revealed the awakening of purpose.

"Yes," she said at last, looking steadily in his face, "promises are sacred and ought to be binding; I have done wrong. I said when the house was finished I would come, and now the house is finished and I will come. Give me only a month for preparation; then you may set the day yourself, and I will marry you."

Other men might have thrown into an extravagance of language their stress of feeling; long habits of repression silenced Allan Brong. In all violent emotion a subtle incredulity lurks that robs it of expression, and the young man might well be a little incredulous of this sudden consent where heretofore had been only temporizing.

"I shall labor to be less unworthy of you," he said, at last. "You are giving up much; now, the world may hold me base in permitting it, and the best devotion of my life may seem but a poor return, but, Jean, you shall have wealth again. I feel, within, the power that is the promise of the future. This is a new country; its opportunities are for him who can seize them, and I can. I can make my way to the front. I will; I must and I will."

The hope and the assurance were borne out in every feature of the strong young face, a face where prematurely the lines of thought were deepening. It was full of that centred expression that belongs to men who from hard buffeting have grown to self-reliance, and Allan Brong had wrestled with the world from youth. His form was wiry and athletic,—no superfluous flesh to retard motion, no flaccid muscles to fail of needed tension; an active, nervous organism, quick of judgment, with faculties right at the surface, with force ready to be launched into each endeavor,—a character to gather strength with urgency. He belonged to the type that develops clever, successful business-men, but men whose energy feeds upon itself and makes impossible a long life.

Now in the elation of confirmed hope he felt the quickening of all his dormant powers, and it was this conscious sense that rang like a prophecy in his "I will; I must and I will."

"Of course you will, Allan," said the young girl, graciously. "Every one allows your cleverness,—every one, that is, but father and Margaret; and even they will be forced to concede it some day," she added, with warmth.

Her lover's face glowed beneath her praise.

"Aren't you afraid of teaching me vanity, sweetheart?"

"How can I teach you what I do not know myself?" she said, naïvely.

They both laughed; happiness effervesces so naturally!

"Then you must set about cultivating it. A woman without vanity is an engine without steam. I shall hang a mirror for you directly."

"You shan't hang it in the parlor," she said, decidedly. "Every one who is obliged to choose between a steel engraving and a chromo compromises on a looking-glass. I don't believe there are six houses here that haven't a looking-glass in the parlor."

" Where will you have it, then ? in the dining-room ?"

" Worse, infinitely. If I must be confronted by my own image, let it at least have the benefit of attitudes. To surprise myself always in the act of eating, to feel that I was nothing but an embodied digestion, would be intolerable."

The fervor with which she pressed her whim had delicious encouragements for her companion. Her little dictates were giving to her promise a blissful reality.

" Eating is such a vulgar necessity, anyway !", she rambled on. " It makes one seem so gross that it takes an excessive daintiness in surroundings to restore one's self-esteem. I am resolved to tolerate within my walls nothing that doesn't minister to the æsthetic. My house shall have nothing cheap or common about it, for I am convinced that half the disordered lives are the product of disordered environments. There's Margaret's, now; what a cheerless place that is ! And do you know, Allan, I don't believe she's as happy as she used to be ?"

The last half of the remark was delivered in a lowered tone of confidence, and the cloud on her lover's face darkened to a scowl.

" Your life will never be like hers," he answered, shortly.

" Oh, no, of course; it never could. But I've made up my mind that her cramped, ugly house has spoiled her good nature. She never wears pretty clothes now, either; and what is more unsuitable than dark dresses in the summer-time ? She might as well take to sun-bonnets at once."

How unconsciously she was pressing the steel into his

flesh! Was the hurt the less that she was unconscious or that the hilt was jewelled? He looked away in silence through the defile of trees. Off from the shelving bank he could see the foliage in shadowed meshes trembling on the water, and catch the low iterative ripple of the stream. There was a vague trouble in his downcast eyes. Was it a misgiving of her content in the only home he could offer? or was it the deeper suspicion that nature had not set her seal of fitness between them? Jean might not understand the cause of his sudden moodiness, but she divined the condition. She was growing aware lately that a mention of her father or Margaret begot a depression in Allan Brong, and she hastened to beguile his thoughts from the morass into which she had unwittingly led them.

But she rose soon, with a perception that it was growing dark. The young man rose also, and, slipping her arm within his own, led her out along the river-bank and took the path back through the woods. As he opened the little gate for her to enter, a sudden motive moved him, for he passed within himself, still retaining her arm.

"Let us go now together, Jean, and tell your father," he said, persuasively. "Or, if it will be any easier, I will go alone."

"Oh, no, no, Allan; not now." With a return of her old vacillating manner, she drew out her arm and waved him back, saying, impatiently, "I will break it to him; leave it to me; leave it to me."

The disappointment in his face was visible across the

darkness, and, half in fear, half in propitiation, she threw her arms about his neck. Her affection had been heretofore only of the receptive kind; this spontaneous abandon thrilled him to subjection.

" When you wish, and as you wish," he said. "I have no will apart from yours."

She lingered a moment in his embrace, then, freeing herself, she hurried into the house, and Allan Brong struck into the woods again, taking the opposite path that led across the town.

CHAPTER III.

AGAIN in the gathering twilight Jean Fennimore might be seen slipping from the stately house and gliding out among the arbored shadows. She moved now more warily than before, and her scrutiny of the windows was sharper; but she passed through the gate unobserved, and took once more the sheltered path that led through the woods to the river.

There was no sprightliness to-night, no dallying with the flowers, no mimicry of the birds; her step was slow, her eyes were cast down in abstraction, and as she moved among the dark boles she seemed someway akin to them, for she was dressed in fullest mourning. She hesitated frequently, and paused, as if about to return; but the impulse was over-borne, and she kept on her way to the rendezvous.

As she reached the angle where the path branched, a hand was laid upon hers, and Allan Brong addressed her.

"I was afraid you weren't coming, Jean, and I had begun to be disappointed," he said.

"I wasn't sure, myself, that I was coming," she answered, evasively.

The words, conjoined to the mood, seemed to disconcert him, and they walked on for a time without speaking. Several weeks had elapsed since they had met before, and, for the first time, sorrow had drawn the unwilling bars and entered the young girl's life. Conversation is wont to halt where trouble broods, and, though her companion sought strenuously an expression of fitting comfort or sympathy, he found none. He could not condole with her: the death of Martin Fennimore had been little deplored by his townsmen; it had been almost welcomed by Allan Brong, and it required an effort to conceal his rebellious gladness. His own insensibility had dulled him to a perception that Jean loved her father, and that his loss must distress her keenly. He thought of her preoccupation only as another phase of a nature moving forever to strange, incalculable tractions, and he sought some harmless channel of diversion.

"I was a little late in coming, myself, to-night," he said. "Saturday is a busy day at the bank, and I stayed to balance the accounts. We are looking for a big rush of business presently, when the mining country is open again. A good many men are beginning to expand stock already, and some are getting their capital loose to operate in the mines. Portland is going to see a big boom now; money'll be plenty; and people that have real estate will do well to avail themselves of the high prices, for booms are treacherous things out here in the West."

He was hardly fortunate. Trade might be the pivot of existence; it was to Allan Brong the stirrup for an expected mount. But to the young girl, it was only an ingenious game that men had invented to keep themselves busy. It neither concerned nor interested her, and she remained silent.

"Where but in Oregon could we get such days?" he ventured again. "Spring in January. The little house looks very cheerful in this sunny weather. I wish the rains were over, so we might have all the days pleasant."

"So do I," she echoed; "our big rooms are so silent and lonesome now. They seem vacant, someway, and the days are all alike. There's no special reason for doing anything; so I don't, and that makes the time longer. Margaret is at the house to-day; she is coming back to live, and I hope the place will be less dreary then."

She did not notice the look of surprised displeasure in her companion's face, and he strove to conceal it as he said, quietly,—

"The place will always be associated to you with memories, I am afraid. Even a plainer home might be a happier one."

"Home! Yes, any place that was home would be happier."

There was no mention of dainty furnishing; the childish disdain was forgotten. Allan Brong saw his misgivings floating away like a mist of the morning. "She has felt the emptiness of shadows," he encouraged himself, "and her need has drawn her to my level." But he said aloud, and his voice was deep and tender,—

"My home has been awaiting you many months, Jean. You are your own mistress now; come, and let us end this hated secrecy. Come with me and be my wife."

She had been resting down against his shoulder, with a

peaceful sense of shelter in its strength; but now she sat erect, and clasped her hands together nervously. She stared for a time upon the ground; then, raising her eyes, she said,—with, he fancied, a touch of repulsion,—

"Don't press me, Allan; don't press me."

The young man was mystified. He could not comprehend such unsteady poises, and he waited for a clue to her mental maze. He caught it when, out of the confusion of her sensations, dropped a fragment of speech,—

"He is dead now."

Yes, he was dead: but what bearing had that upon the matter? Martin Fennimore's burial had opened the way for happiness; why was his shadow lurking at the gate?

"What is it, dear? Tell me what troubles you?"

"His voice was against it, Allan," she faltered. "To the last he said, it would be with me as with the others. I could deny him while he was living, but now—now——" She could say no more. Her lips quivered, but in the revulsion of his own anger the young man was oblivious to her need.

"What accusation did he bring against me?" he demanded. "That I was poor, that was all. Against my character, against my life, he could say nothing. Is it a crime to be poor? The money he thought to leave you, it was found at his death, was gone, for the "Dermott" lead was barren, and you, Jean,—you are poor, too."

There was a ring of satisfaction in the announcement, as though her loss was an added sanction to his claim: and his words seemed to carry an argument, for she sat in deep thought. When she lifted her eyes again the fluctuating light had left them, and some of the old placidity had returned.

"I don't care for the money: I'd quite forgot it," she said. "And yet that ought to make a difference. Father surely couldn't expect me to marry wealth when I had none myself."

"You have the house yet,—that is considerable; and the ranch,—that will be worth something in time. You are still the richest, and I wish you had nothing, nothing," he said, passionately.

"I have very little, and I think now father must be reconciled, for he must know."

"Yes, I am sure, I am quite sure he is reconciled."

She leaned her cheek upon his arm, and there was silence. For a time the gulf that had opened between them was bridged, and they were back in the old era of content. But not for long. Soon she raised her head; some thought had broken its moorings and was drifting away, dragging her convictions after it out to the troubled sea again. In his anxious alertness, the other felt it immediately.

"What is it?" he asked.

"Oh, Allan! how can I tell you! It wasn't only the poverty he opposed: it was you, it was you, yourself."

The young man's eyes gleamed with sudden rage; then through the rage shot a look that was undeniably fear,—a strange terror that slowly overcame the anger. Where her head was bowed, Jean could not see the expression of her lover's face, but she felt the cording muscle in his arm and the strong throbbing of his heart.

" How can I speak?" he said, with quick energy. " He was your father, and he is dead; what can I say? I did not know his dislike was a personal matter, and yet what was it—forgive me if I wound you—what was it but another instance of his despotism? Amelia married; he cast her off; Margaret married; he disowned her. I had not your advantages in education, for he had instructed you carefully. You had every opportunity; I had none, and he hated me for my misfortunes. It was my sin that I was poor, and that I loved you; but, Jean, it was my right and my privilege as well."

"I love you," she asserted. It was a quiet assurance that her father's prejudices had not infected her,—nay, that his harshness had rather impelled her to a warmer championship. The young man's vehement resentment had served for the time to vindicate their relation and confound her scruples. Still, notwithstanding her graciousness and her mild acceptance of the old conditions, Allan Brong felt that the past was not restored. The tone of subtle defiance in which she used to confess her father's opposition; the look of straight resolve with which she announced that she would choose like the others, and give up her inheritance rather than her lover, these were missing to-night, and the young man knew the meaning. She could defy a living father, but the dead had an authority she could not shake. It filled him with dread, a dread which turned him sick; if now,

now that the last obstacle was removed, she had come under the spell of Martin Fennimore's tyranny, and was going to forsake him!—he rose and paced hurriedly to and fro. And Jean rose also, and taking his hand led him mechanically along the homeward path. As they reached the gate, she stepped forward to open it, but he drew her violently to him.

"You will kill me, you will kill me," he said. But she did not speak; she only lingered a moment beside him, then without a word she slipped through the gate and was gone.

CHAPTER IV.

JEAN FENNIMORE'S mind was scarcely less disturbed than her lover's. Ever present was the knowledge of her father's disapproval, made forcible now by the memory of their last interview. She had condensed her courage into a moment of strength, had gone and told him her purpose, and he had received her in a fury. His outburst had been fortunately interrupted by the announcement of a messenger who had come riding in haste from the distant gold-fields. That messenger was closeted all the day with Martin Fennimore,—all the day and late into the night. After he left, the old man had remained alone for a time and then had summoned his daughter.

How every event of that night had burned itself into her thoughts! How the scene was limned upon her memory! The black background of book-lined walls, the fire smouldering in the grate, the deep, richly-carved chair in which her father was sitting with his head supported against his hand, and close beside him on the heavy table the private chest wherein was kept—he had told her often—his will, that left the legacy of all his wealth to her. It was a constantly-recurring picture now; and his tones, gentle and tender,—how they clung to her ears! He did not speak of disinheritance to-night; there was no trace of anger at her

28

disobedience, only a hungering desire to rescue her from some imminent catastrophe. He urged his appeal with a fervor almost of remorse, as though something made her sacrifice imperative. And still, despite her pity and her affection (for she loved the stoic old man), she had refused to promise. No entreaty could wring from her an assurance that she would give up Allan Brong. Yet when she rose to go, her father had no word of reproach, but drew her to his heart and kissed her tenderly. So they had parted; and in the morning Martin Fennimore was sitting in the same place, dead.

Between Jean and her father had existed a sympathy that was covert but real; for she could probe to where, under the cold, repellent surface, his heart beat humanly. Her union with him was closer than that of her sisters had ever been, for there was not alone affection, but recognition and faith as well.

When, long before, he had realized her dreaded attachment, and had reasoned with her, somehow, though she was silent, and would give no pledge of fidelity, he trusted her, as he had not trusted either of the others. There was something in Jean responsive to his heart's cry, however much she might try to deaden it. For days after his appeals, the elastic gayety that dashed her natural moods was gone, and the father knew that she was thinking. Slight thread, this, to hold the hope of a life, yet Martin Fennimore anchored all his trust to that frail answering chord. He felt that in this child there was something that was his, something that would yet move to the magnet of his will.

But it was only as might be expected, that Jean should be drawn to Allan Brong. His poverty conjured in her no grim presentiments, for she held still the glorious dowry of innocence. And when did sordid thoughts stir the pure pulse of youth? and when did difficulty daunt its courage, or fear appall its hope? His poverty but helped to inspire in her a deeper sentiment of romance. Yet any one but Martin Fennimore would willingly have linked a daughter's destiny to that of Allan Brong. Indeed, the general sentiment was, that the day was not far off when the perverse old man might hold himself favored in having such a son-in-law. Alas! Martin Fennimore had died too soon,— too soon, was it? or too late?—and he had left to his daughter, in the irony of fortune, a heritage of poverty and the deathless memory of his prejudice.

CHAPTER V.

ONE might suppose that with the restraint of her father's presence removed, Jean would have avowed the purpose, which she certainly retained, of marrying Allan Brong, and have received his attentions openly. But two forces still held her irresolute,—the unsteady element in her own nature, that like restless waves tossed her mind about till her will propelled it to the harbor of a decision; and her sister Margaret, who with her husband and child had returned to the home of her girlhood.

Margaret Wright was, in character, almost a counterpart of Martin Fennimore. She had all his pride and love of power, though his taciturn temper was counteracted in her by a love of social intercourse. It was inevitable that Margaret's strong, incisive character should rule the negative nature of her sister, and that Jean should yield her much of the provisional obedience she had yielded her father. Strangely, although Margaret had defied the autocrat herself, he had no fiercer champion in his purposes than his discarded daughter. Perhaps she had not estimated the old man's obstinacy when she took her own fatal step; perhaps the failure of her married life had taught her wisdom. Whatever the cause, the father's opposition to Allan Brong had descended to his daughter, and she was not likely to prove a passive opponent.

When next in the gray twilight Jean stole down the broad staircase to the side door, suddenly a hand was on the knob and Margaret stood before her.

"You are going to meet Allan Brong," she said, fastening her keen gray eyes upon the culprit.

"Yes," Jean stammered. No thought of denial came to her, though the charge seemed such a serious one as Margaret uttered it; and without a protest she followed where her sister led the way to the parlor.

"I suspected your interviews before father died," Margaret observed, closing the door leisurely and seating herself, "but I had thought decency would have restrained you since."

Jean stood in silence beside the grate. Her sister's tone was lending to her act an aspect of guilt, and the instinct of defence was rousing her aggressiveness.

"A little regard for a parent's wishes might have been more decorous in a daughter," said Margaret, icily.

"Regard for his wishes never seemed to have restrained you much," Jean retorted, sharply.

She regretted immediately her savage thrust. A look of pain crossed Margaret's face,—Margaret whom nothing could humble,—and when she spoke it was in a tone that was striving after calmness:

"No, nothing restrained me,—pride, nor reason, nor self-respect, nothing,—nothing."

It was a sullen avowal, and she winced visibly under the arraignment. But she shook her head as though tossing off her self-reproach, and said, in an accent of imperious resignation,—

"He was a good father to us, Jean. However harsh to the world, he was unselfish and devoted to his family. We owed him obedience. I see it now; I could not see it then. Do you think I gained anything by abandoning him? Where is the comfort, the power, the honor I had once?—I, Margaret Wright, the consort of the poor and the ignorant, with whom in my infatuation I cast my lot!"

She was being beguiled out of her wonted calmness. The remembrance of her folly was awakening an undue excitement. But the face of the listener was unmoved. No consonant chord had been struck, and the young girl's attitude betrayed a half-concealed impatience.

"I should think you could bear such things," she said, coldly, "for love."

"For love!" There was a ring of scorn in the words. "For love, indeed! And yet,—yes, my heart used to plead so too once. I was absorbed in my affection. It seemed a choice between my love and vacancy, for I couldn't picture a future that would be supportable without his presence. Every idea was swallowed up in my infatuation. And Caleb was the same; he indulged also in the pretty illusions, but——" Margaret hesitated; she shrank from laying bare to her sister the failure of her life. And yet that warning was the only hope left of disenchanting Jean; and she said, slowly, "When respect goes, love soon follows. The chivalry we see in men dwells but too often in our own fancy.

c

In my case, senseless eccentricity and shiftless indifference
are the realities out of which the last atom of romance has
vanished. Father judged truly; I left him, and for what?
A husband I despise, and a child whose future is hourly a
goad to regret."

Jean was gazing idly upon the floor. Somehow she could
not appreciate the disgrace or the wretchedness of Margaret's alliance; precept and example had slipped from her
mind without leaving an impression. Her quiet, dispassionate manner nettled her companion, who said, somewhat
irritably,—

"You are deluding yourself with the thought that my
experience cannot come to you, and you are putting away
your influence and position as not essential to your happiness. But father did not so regard them; he held money
to be of value and——"

The young girl looked slowly up. "He sees it all
differently now, Allan says. He knows how little anything
counts but love."

"Allan says! Allan! that nothing counts but love!
Probably, also, he is clever enough to add that no love
counts but his own. I suppose he has convinced you that
no one else could be induced to wed Martin Fennimore's
daughter,—to wed her, let alone to throw any money into
the bargain. Well, husbands are scarce here, particularly
husbands of such quality! I trust you have thanked him
prettily for his condescension, for surely Mr. Brong pur-
chases your inheritance dear when he pays for it—his love!"

She laughed, a cynical laugh that cut her sister to the heart. Margaret's sarcasm was always her best weapon, because the other had no foil. The weaker nature recoiled from the stabs, but could not thrust back. The accusations seemed too cruel to be answered.

"Oh, Margaret! Margaret!" she faltered.

"It seems to me," Margaret went on, mercilessly, "a touch of self-esteem might be seemly in your Allan, if he could be induced to assume it. Modesty sits well upon the plebs; but a certain grand air of arrogance is rather demanded of the aristocracy. He does not realize his worth. The selfishness of your father, who spent his life acquiring for you, is a cold contrast to his nobility. *He* would not sully his love with lucre, but gives it to you pure and priceless in its native poverty. What a poor pitiful contempt he must cherish for the aims and labors of Martin Fennimore!"

Jean felt keenly that it was all wrong. Margaret's assumptions were false, her lover's attitude was caricatured, his sentiments perverted; but defend him she could not. She was as powerless under her sister's lash as though it were of thongs; still, though for the moment she quailed, she was not convinced, for the glow in her eyes only deepened as Margaret ended,—

"Such a hero is worthy of your best worship. His character is holy, his motives are exalted, and a father's will is a very slight thing to sacrifice on the altar of—his love."

Jean swept a helpless glance about the room in search of something that might offer an escape, and her eyes were suddenly arrested on the opposite wall. A life-size portrait of Martin Fennimore, taken in his youth, was hanging there, and the rays of the setting sun shifting upward, fell athwart the painted face and lit it into life. The picture had never been considered a true one; the gentleness of the countenance was a libel on the stern old man. But now Jean saw with a startled pleasure what a perfect likeness it was. She knew that expression; it had filled his face the night of their last meeting, and death had surprised and frozen it there. That was the look he wore when she left him, the look that was sealed under the coffin-lid. As she watched, the canvas seemed slowly growing into the personal presence of her father; the eyes were fixed upon hers, and the lips were parted to address her. Margaret glanced across, and like an inspiration came a thought.

"Is he nothing to you?" she said, with quiet reproach, "the dead,—the father who carried into eternity every feeling that moved him in life."

Jean did not reply; but her eyes continued fixed on her father, and across her lip passed almost imperceptibly a tremor.

"The love that had sufficed for three was all given to you, Jean. Because the echo of his footstep is heard no longer in the house, is he gone out of his children's lives? Because his voice is hushed in an eternal silence, is its sound forgotten? His life was a hard, desolate one; the springs of feeling were choked by early suffering, and never flowed freely again; and the coldness of his manner the world returned in coldness of heart, so that no kindly remembrance of him lingers in the minds of his fellows. His memory shall be cherished nowhere if not in his home. And the hope of his life was centred in you. I was gone, disowned, an out-cast, but you were still dear to him. Our father carried to our mother the recognition of but one child, and that was you."

The listener's mouth was taking on wavering curves, her figure had lost some of its resolute poise, and was leaning against the mantel.

"Did time lessen his opposition to Allan Brong?" Margaret went on. "Wasn't the last request that passed his lips an appeal to you to give him up? Believe me, to parents is given a clearer vision than we ever know. Some day, God grant it may not be when too late, you will recognize that your father's last prayer was sped with a knowledge beyond the human."

She had touched the chord at last; tears stood in the dark, upturned eyes, and the slight, girlish frame was shaken with sobs; but Margaret did not try to soothe her.

"Better to weep now, now while you can yet turn back, and be reconciled to him, than to weep when even in the grave he shall cast you off. The curse of a living father is a terrible thing,—I must carry this through life; but the curse of a dead father,—oh, Jean! Jean! do not draw that upon your head."

4

The doomed girl was bending like a reed to the tumult of emotions. The last trace of resistance was vanishing from her face. She was wretched, miserable, past the power of words; and she did not speak,—only swayed to and fro. She was being conquered. Her form drooped helplessly, but her eyes remained fixed on the eyes that watched her from the wall. It seemed as though some subtle influence in them rather than in her sister's words was mastering her will and forcing her to subjection.

"You avoided a rupture with him always," Margaret continued. "You lulled him with a deceptive hope. You had not the courage to brave the living, but you will defy the dead."

"Oh, no, no!" she called, brokenly. "Spare me! Spare me!"

"He trusted you, Jean," Margaret said, in a voice so low it was almost a whisper. "In spite of your own acts, he trusted you. His will—did he not leave that unchanged, bequeathing you all as a pledge of his faith? You have accepted his home, you have taken all he had left; and now, now that he is helpless, you will betray him."

"No, no, I will not!" she cried in distress. "I will be true; I will be true!"

A gleam of triumph lit up the face of Margaret Wright, but the low earnestness was unbroken.

"His blessing shall rest upon you, dear; do not falter. His words are in your ears; his prayer, that death has deepened to a command, is echoing in your heart; he calls you from the grave to do his bidding. Go now, and end all with Allan Broug."

She passed quietly through the parlor and opened the front door. Jean shrank back, and raised her clasped hands to her father; but no word came from the painted lips, no sign from the rigid brow. She looked from his fixed eyes to her sister's; but the gaze that met hers was merciless, and blindly, mechanically, she moved to the door. Slowly, with unsteady feet, she passed down the stone steps, across the lawn, through the arched gate-way, and, like one in a dream, took the open road to the river.

CHAPTER VI.

THE interview had occupied considerable time, but, as Jean came slowly along, there in the old place she could discern the outlines of a man's figure. His face was in profile, and he was watching the path that led through the woods. As she advanced, a twig snapped beneath her feet; he turned, and, perceiving her, hastened forward.

She was striving to collect her faculties and compose herself, but the pleased welcome of his manner unnerved her efforts, and burying her face in her hands she turned away.

It had come at last,—he felt it instantly,—this that had haunted him for weeks, that came to him in the darkness with its grim foreboding, though he fought it off with all the fierceness of his nature. To-night was his last; henceforth she would be lost to him; he saw it with the quick intuition of fear, and he strained her to his breast with voiceless energy.

He did not attempt to caress her. He asked but one question, "Are you going to be my wife?" and she answered, "No." That was all. It never occurred to him to reason or plead; what had the months been but pleading and reasoning? He understood the contradictory impulses of her being, and the strength of the superstitious power

40

that was moving her. He knew that the dead held her soul in a grasp the living was powerless to shake off.

For a long time he held her. His mouth was rigid; his clasp was firm, as though it would defy the world,—alas! it was not the world with which he battled. His gray eyes, in the dusk, shot out faint jets of light; in his face was a concentrated struggle which told that the energies of his nature were in mortal combat, and that many were fighting to the death. At last he turned, caught her hand firmly within his own, and, saying only " Come," took the path back through the woods, across the narrow strip of town to its farther edge.

There in the midst of a clearing stood a cottage; he opened the door and led her in. This was the little house that with his own hands, patiently, laboriously, he had built. He had spoken often of their home, but to-night for the first time Jean Fennimore had crossed its threshold. In each room a lamp hung suspended. He drew them down and lit them, then, coming back, he grasped her wrist and led her forward.

It was an unpretentious place, a humble little cottage, yet love lent a grace to simplicity. Everything was inexpensive, but the pervading harmony bespoke a refined taste. The floors of the parlor and adjoining bedroom were carpeted with skins, coyote chiefly (for these could be had for a trifle from the Indians), into whose softness the feet sank pleasantly. A home-made lounge stood in one corner, and beside the window a softly-padded seat commanded the magnificent outlook across the distant hills. The archway into the dining-room was a net-work of clinging vines, and flowers were blooming about in the luxuriance that the climate favored.

From the stationary sideboard to the little foot-rest that waited beside the grate, everything attested how the mind of the worker had gone into the details of this home, and how the thought of this girl had wrought itself into nerve and sinew. The long patience of his love could find no voice to equal their dumb eloquence.

As they advanced Allan Brong's agitation deepened visibly. The sight of his home now never to be hers was maddening him. A vase stood in one of the windows wherein was blossoming a delicate forget-me-not. He seized it, opened the door, and hurled it out without a word.

"Allan! Allan!" the young girl pleaded, resting her hand upon his arm; but he shook it off impatiently.

"You pity the broken flower," he cried, fiercely, "and the shattered vase, but my shattered life is nothing to you."

He grasped her arm and paced the floor again. He was beside himself. The glow in his eyes was unnaturally bright, and the hectic flush of his cheek revealed the fever that was raging within. Both felt dimly that his despair had for the time mastered his reason. As he walked his grip upon her arm was very painful, and she called out, feebly,—

"You are hurting me, Allan."

"Hurting you! You can feel? You know pain? Pain of the body, a little pressure of the arm, that is suffering to you; but the crushing of the soul,—bah! the Fennimores were always soulless. Who doesn't know that? But," he spoke with the sudden recklessness of resolve, "they can suffer, and they shall. Oh, Martin Fennimore, you have hated me; you have hated me, and you have robbed me; but I shall rob you too, and my hate, like yours, shall be pitiless."

CHAPTER VII.

SINCE the discovery of the worthlessness of Martin Fennimore's effects, it had been gradually impressed upon the minds of both his daughters that some new provision must be made for Jean's support. The ranch might in time be valuable, but it was unproductive now, and this with the house was all that remained of her father's fortune. The one source of income must therefore be made available, and a tenant be sought for the Fennimore place.

The spring had opened early, and the great rush to the gold-fields had set in. Portland was teeming with men, ocean-steamers from San Francisco were making regular and frequent trips, the population had doubled, and brick blocks lined the business streets, every store taken by some enterprising company competing for the profits of the sudden trade. A brisk navigation opened too, along the Columbia, and daily river steamers were leaving the crowded wharves laden with men and freight for the upper country. The old pioneers looked for a moment aghast at the horde of barbarians sweeping in upon the town, but the excitement was infectious; soon the first settlers had plunged into the new methods and were at the crest of the advancing wave. There could be no difficulty, therefore, in securing a good revenue from the Fennimore place.

44

At this time it became also clear to Margaret that some new provision must be made for the maintenance of the Wright family. Her last jewel was gone. The clothes that had constituted her wardrobe when she left home were fast outgrowing service, and she could not see how in the nature of things, and the nature of Caleb Wright, they were ever likely to be replaced. Something must be done, and that something she must do herself.

There was an active revolving of plans in the proud woman's mind, a holding of them up at angles the better to catch effects, and a setting of them off at distances for impersonal contemplation. But it was hard to look dispassionately out of her haughty eyes, or to survey as an uninterested spectator what concerned her so intimately. All plans for self-support were degrading; she could only question which seemed to least compromise her dignity and the name of her father; and she chose what the time and the public condition promised to make very remunerative,— a fashionable boarding-house.

The thought of resigning her home to strangers had, for some reason, become very unwelcome to its young mistress, so when Mrs. Wright proposed to lease the house and leave her in possession of her own apartments, the offer was joyously accepted. The family dignities did not seem to weigh much upon Jean. She was impervious to an idea that patronage could reflect discredit upon the Fennimore pretensions.

The necessity was dire that could impel Margaret Wright

into the position of caterer to remunerative guests, but, once committed, her name was a pledge of superior things. And as accommodations were scarce, and the place was itself confessedly the handsomest in the town, it was not remarkable that almost before it opened the house was filled with Portland's aristocracy. Frederick Rand was there, the portly banker; not the Crœsus that the title usually suggests, still a man of ample and increasing wealth. Mr. Gibbon, the Episcopal divine, and his wife came next; then Thomas Todd, the druggist; jovial Harry Price, the editor of the town daily; and other men of standing in the community.

Mrs. Wright's venture was insured against social lesion in the quality of her guests; she gave it a further security in her own personal bearing, for she wore her dignity like an ægis, at once a defence and a decoration. Her cold, calm presence was self-assertive. It was impossible to treat that superb creature as anything other than a high and mighty potentate. One felt it a privilege to share her presence, and she made it, by her efficiency, a privilege to share the excellence of her table and the elegance of her home. And now once more Mrs. Wright took her station among the elect, and held it henceforth with an undisputed title.

CHAPTER VIII.

It was shortly after the establishment of the new system that one morning, when the rest of the household had finished breakfast, Frederick Rand, in an epicure's immunities, still lingered with Mrs. Wright over his salmon-steak and coffee.

"That fellow Richards," he was saying,—"you may have heard of him, for he is a town character,—here a while ago he grub-staked an old miner going up into Idaho, and now, he tells me, the lucky rascal has struck a rich thing on a placer. That's compounding to a purpose."

"Well, some one ought to gain," Mrs. Wright, observed; "there are enough already who have lost. My family can hardly be expected to cherish much enthusiasm for the country."

"If your father hadn't been so dead set after quartz, Mrs. Wright; if he'd just gone in for placers, he'd have been all right. It was quartz that wrecked him. He was, as your husband would say, a victim to the non-existent. And, the engineer tells me, he insisted upon sinking, even after the lead was proved barren. He had singular ideas sometimes, —Mr. Fennimore."

"Father was guided by his own convictions," she answered, curtly. "He wasn't the kind to seek opinions of

47

his neighbors. And his judgment never erred,—except perhaps in this one case, which chanced to entail rather serious consequences; though that, of course, was no arraignment of his rare good sense."

The banker smiled. Mrs. Wright's intolerance was clearly hereditary.

" Certainly, business reverses must be expected in every man's career," he said; " or, rather, it is a remarkably-directed career that succeeds in escaping them."

Mrs. Wright smiled in her turn, for the banker's self-gratulation was very transparent.

" You are not going to hazard your record by indulging in mining ventures ?" she questioned, suspiciously.

" Not while there are so many ready to dispose of their town lots. I am content to enjoy the mines vicariously, as long as the miscreants leave me the certainty and hustle off to the chances. Well, man's choice is free; if his head is filled with batter in place of brains, he must expect his pudding to be a little thin. Now, here a couple of months ago, I bought that vacant block down by the river. To-day it is needed for dockage, and triples the investment. That was Brong's speculation. By the way," he said, in abrupt transition, " I can't understand what has come over Allan of late. He isn't at all the fellow he was a little while back. I have been thinking possibly your sister has something to do with it. Will you pardon my inquiring if there is any trouble between them ?"

Mrs. Wright was not unwilling to announce publicly that

the family was to be spared the disgrace of another poor alliance.

"Yes, Jean has given up her idea of marrying Mr. Brong," she said, tersely. "Father opposed the union,—he thought it unsuitable, and I am sure sister will be the happier for being guided by his judgment."

"Poor fellow! he's taking it badly, very badly," said the banker, sympathetically.

Allan Brong was taking it badly, and no mistake. This man,—whom secretly mothers appropriated by transferring to him their son's lineaments; whom openly fathers held before the same sons, as an embodiment of what a young man could be,—Allan Brong had been carried home in a stupor of intoxication one night, and since had given himself over to a prolonged round of dissipation.

Every one was surprised and shocked. But when, through Frederick Rand, the cause became known, there was not a man in the town but felt that some one was chargeable with Allan Brong's downfall.

Martin Fennimore had had his neighbors' dislike in life; now he had their condemnation. Mrs. Wright, too, was accorded her share of criticism; and even Jean for the moment ceased to be a fellow-victim and became a criminal agent.

But when in their zeal of sympathy his friends ventured a censure of her action, Allan Brong waved them into silence. "The fault is mine," he insisted, "only mine."

He would shield her still, for his chivalry remained even

c   d   5

in his debasement. Yet when liquor had relaxed his self-control, he raved wickedly against old Martin Fennimore, for his tyranny; against Margaret, for abetting him; against Jean, even, who had promised and then denied him. But most bitterly he raved against himself for some terrible wrong that his fancy linked with her rejection. But only in his intoxication did he allude to the past; when sober, he walked as in a stupor.

It became apparent to Frederick Rand as the weeks and the months went by that Allan Brong's usefulness was at an end. He did his work faithfully still; the faculties worked mechanically in the old groove, and his accounts showed the same careful accuracy; but the mental power that had made him as a staff to his master, the keen sagacity, the quick, unerring judgment,—these were gone, and, the banker suspected, gone forever.

Still, he determined to wait. A reconciliation might be effected between the lovers, or time might restore the young man's vigor. He had suffered some amatory pangs himself in the course of his experience, the rich man would allow, and had felt disposed to retaliate upon that nearest embodiment of fate, his own comfortable person, but he had done nothing rash, and time had proved an opiate for his aches,— why not for Allan Brong's? And the temporary interval of dissipation Frederick Rand could wink at. He was not prepared to deny that he had himself indulged occasionally upon slighter provocation. Yes, he could overlook that; Allan Brong was too valuable to be lost while there was any hope.

And Jean,—Jean, who with blithest feet had tripped along her days, a delicate-winged humming-bird, poising now here, now there, sipping joy from everything,—Jean, the spirit of airiness,—what had transformed her? Her laugh was no longer the careless, volatile thing that belonged to her years. She avoided festivities, she shunned even the sociability of her sister's parlor, till it came to be suspected by the inmates of the house that the gentle Jean, not the queenly Margaret, was the one who felt the humiliation of guests.

But they forgave her aloofness in pity for the misery that spoke from her young face.

"This rupture with Allan Brong is affecting her health," they whispered. "Her love dies hard. It is touching, her loyalty to that flinty old father."

Yet when, in the solitude of her own room, she flung herself upon a couch, or paced the floor in agitation, her reproaches did not savor much of love. The affection, one might fancy, had become metamorphosed into hate, so fierce was the glare in her dark eyes.

Had she lost youth's glamorous faith? Had she found in her idol's gold some base alloy? Oh, for a power that could unclasp the girdle of the flesh with all its deceptive guises! And oh, for a pity in the world that would leave a human soul its trust! Nature with gentle hand woos our confidence in a sympathy so fine we see, as in childhood we saw in our mother's eyes, our own exact reflection. The mountains took on to Jean a sentient shade, and the skies behind the sun-glare were only a hollow void.

CHAPTER IX.

"MRS. WRIGHT," observed the druggist's wife, as one day in late summer the family sat at breakfast, "you are looking unwell this morning; really, quite unwell. Mr. Todd and I fancied we heard you moving about considerably in the night. Were you ill?"

"I was somewhat restless," the hostess allowed. "I tried to inveigle sleep by a little pedestrian exercise, but I was hardly successful. I am rather subject to spells of wakefulness. I hope, though, my walking did not produce the same condition in you?"

"Oh, no," Mr. Todd, assured her. "I had forgotten that we heard you. I guess there wasn't more than one brain-cell awake, and that one didn't have its eyes open. But Mrs. Todd, here, sees and hears in her sleep as distinctly as when she is awake."

"Why, Mr. Todd!" said his wife, chidingly.

"Do you know, Mrs. Wright," the rector observed, "this morning is the first time I have noticed a resemblance between you and Miss Fennimore?"

The universal gaze was directed to Jean, who tried to raise her head indifferently, as became such a harmless notice; but her eyes remained fastened on her plate, and a hot blush contended with the pallor of her cheek.

"A family headache," said Mrs. Wright, relieving her confusion, " must beget a family likeness. The resemblance will probably vanish with the ache."

"It is this fitful state of health in woman that so limits her usefulness," Mr. Wright observed, blandly, to the rector. Whenever the conversation languished, Mrs. Wright's husband felt it incumbent upon him as host to revive it immediately. If his remarks leaned always in one fatal direction, that was perhaps accidental. " Instability in the physical lends instability to thought," he went on, discursively; " for a sound mind is the prerogative of health. Have you ever stopped to think, Mr. Gibbon, that an eminent philosopher has never appeared among the ranks of womankind? Woman's emotional nature is always a bias; the shackles of self keep her from that eagle flight wherein the mind can look dispassionately; and truth, which is to man an abstract entity, an intellectual end, is to woman but a related condition, whose end is—what? a quickening of feeling. It is this sensational element that makes me regret my daughter's not being born a boy. She cannot follow the line of my labors; she cannot cut a swath across the world of thought; she is a creature of limitations. It is a sad thing, Mr. Gibbon, to be disappointed in an only child."

"Indeed! indeed! I am sorry," stammered the good man, looking helplessly to his wife, and then to the other members at the table. But the amused persecutors left him to his fate,—all but Mr. Price, who with malign mischief hastened to encourage the philosopher.

"But," he said, "I fail to see the need for thinkers of our race if, as you hold, original thought and investigation is no longer possible to us. I had acquitted myself of all responsibility, and I was getting ready to abdicate in favor of your *protégé*, the Indian."

"Ah, but he must be taught how to utilize his conditions, Mr. Price. He must know what to look for, and he must be made to feel the tremendous importance of the work he is to do for the world. Think, my friend; for untold ages man has been living and passing away without being able to arrive at the first principles of the constitution of mind, and now the red race is becoming extinct, and the last hope of settling it is vanishing with them. We must seize the opportunity; we must rouse the Indian to glance once into his inner mechanism; we must wring from him before he goes this perishing secret."

It was rarely that Mr. Wright was permitted this license of speech, for his wife had a sleuth's scent for his foible, and managed generally to head it off in conversation; but she had excused herself now, in view of her indisposition, and Caleb was rioting at will.

"But what element in the Indian character particularly fits him, in your judgment, for the investigation of philosophy?" asked the editor.

He rose as he questioned, and, with a sly wink at the clergyman, passed out of the room. But Mr. Wright accepted his departure with smiling equanimity, and addressed his reply with equal enthusiasm to the minister.

"What element, Mr. Gibbon? you ask what element? Every element, sir, every attribute of the complete Indian. Original thought is possible to any race only at its dawn, and nations have heretofore all been victims of civilization. The Greeks—the nearest approach we have to original thinkers—were they not spoiled for philosophic uses by the coming in of Egyptian and Asiatic ideas? History saw its boldest thought in the early life of Greece, but she was of too absorptive a nature to keep the isolation that was needed. Now civilization slips off an Indian harmless; the two cannot assimilate. Culture is to the savage a thing so uncongenial that even the merest rudiments of learning refuse to adhere. The Red man, thank heaven! can still claim the title of untutored, despite the senseless efforts of the government to ruin him for his mission. The Indian," he continued, "will bring to his task no preconceptions or prejudices. His mind is a beautiful, untouched blank. He possesses the *nóos* as simple as a child's, yet withal he has the keen, unerring physical sight which is a pledge of the mental, and an obstinacy which will insure firmness in results. I tell you, Mr. Gibbon, the attitude of the American people to the mission of the Indian is the knavish attitude of Jacob the supplanter; it is the arrogance of the Egyptian who refuses to see in subject Israel a chosen people. And I say there must arise another Moses who shall turn back the flood of Egyptian power and corruption and leave this isolated remnant of that same grand race to work out its allotted destiny."

As Caleb Wright paused for breath, he noted, what had escaped him before, that the members of the family, having finished breakfast, had all withdrawn, and that Mrs. Wright, led back perhaps by a divination, was standing beside his chair. Had he glanced up sooner, Mr. Gibbon might have remained unenlightened as to some of the purposes in creation, for Mrs. Wright's presence had a depressing influence on her husband's eloquence. As it was, he hastened to push back his chair, remarking, apologetically,—

"I didn't notice that I was detaining you, Mr. Gibbon. You are too appreciative a listener for your own economy of time."

"I hadn't noticed particularly that I was being detained," said the minister. And he wondered, as he withdrew, if his affability atoned for his little violence to truth.

Caleb Wright looked askance at his wife, expecting her accustomed censure for this lapse, or rather relapse, into the Indian problem. It was a forbidden theme, but Caleb was liable to recurrent spells of forgetfulness in which his mind plunged into the living issue with an enthusiasm born of suppression. But Margaret forgot her reproof this morning. She seemed preoccupied, and, after giving her orders for the day, withdrew to her own room.

She did not occupy it alone, however, for Jean shared her privacy, and seemed even more ailing than her sister; certainly she was the most constrained and abstracted.

Mrs. Wright's headache next morning was no better; in fact, it appeared a little worse.

"You must let me prepare something for you," said the druggist; these nervous headaches make life a nightmare." But the ache refused to be spirited away by drugs. Indisposition settled into illness, and Mrs. Wright's health became to her friends a subject of daily inquiry.

The malady was surely unique in its nature, for the best skill in the place failed to shake it. Indeed, such skill as the town afforded seemed incompetent to even decide satisfactorily what the trouble was; for the physician generalized it vaguely as an affection of the nerves,—a diagnosis which Mrs. Wright scouted without mercy.

At last, in an outburst of sturdy disgust, the imperious lady announced that she would remain no longer the victim of Portland's medical ignorance, but would take the very next steamer for San Francisco. Being a woman of decision, she impressed her erudite husband forthwith into the service of packing, and two days later, reclining in her invalid's chair, Mrs. Wright was waving her adieus from the deck of the "Syphax."

It had been her avowed intention to take a nurse, and leave Jean as a sort of assistant director in her absence; but at the last moment the plan was changed. The nurse was dismissed, and Mrs. Wright was accompanied to San Francisco by her sister.

CHAPTER X.

THE month allotted for Mrs. Wright's absence passed uneventfully. The gentlemen were occupied with increased business, and the ladies with settling the social status of the wives of new-comers. They missed Mrs. Wright's nice discernment in the matter of aspirants, and were desiring her now especially in the question of a certain late arrival, whose assumptions they were pleased to consider somewhat out of proportion to her husband's bank account.

"What do you hear from below?" asked the druggist's wife, of Mr. Wright, while the subject was being agitated. "Is Mrs. Wright better? She expected to be getting back by this time, didn't she?"

"Well, yes; maybe she rather hoped to. I think not unlikely she did express something to that effect," he answered, hesitatingly. "But there's no telling, there's no telling."

Caleb was showing an unwonted reticence on the subject of his wife's illness, and reticence was a germ of very recent development in his nature. Still, it was hardly strange that he should be a trifle erratic with no wife about to regulate his habits of mind.

One theme there was, however, that he was always willing to discuss, upon which he was always primed, and he chuckled mentally at the lawless liberty with which he was debating it in his wife's absence. No member of the family had escaped. From Frederick Rand to the old housekeeper, each separately and all collectively had been regaled upon the pressing call of philosophy and the mission of the Indian. But the subject was a self-feeder, and now, turning from Mrs. Todd and her inquiries, he directed himself to the minister, upon whose Christian forbearance he could count as longest suffering, and renewed the conversation of yesterday.

"You have never, I believe, Mr. Gibbon, had brought to your attention the peculiar mental characteristics of the Indian. The Indians now are a wonderfully reflective people when you come to know them. They are not like us, a race of talkers, but are silent and self-contained, speaking rarely and then in few words. This meditative tendency of the mind is something unique. I have watched an Indian squatted upon the ground, gazing into vacancy for hours together. Now, did you ever detect a white man in the act? Even in your own limited observation of the aborigines, you must have noticed something of this. At the overland way-stations have you not seen ten or a dozen of them standing around, holding their blankets about them while an almost Afric sun beat down upon their uncovered heads? The whites are in the shelter of the wretched station-house, chattering like magpies, but the dignified native is standing lost in contemplation. You have noted, I am sure, at such times, the solemn expression, the thoughtful, almost pensive shade in their steady gaze, the silence of thoughts too profound for words. And when the train moved on and you turned for a last glance, you saw them standing in the same spot, gazing at the deserted track, waiting for their minds in a natural sequence to revert to locomotion. I never behold the stately figures, the calm, stoic faces, so in contrast with the rushing, babbling whites, but I blush,—I blush, Mr. Gibbon, for my color and my race."

Mr. Gibbon seemed disposed to blush a little himself, just that moment, not so much because of his color and race, perhaps, as because of an observation he heard the banker offer *sotto voce* to his neighbor, to the effect that, if Mrs. Wright didn't get back soon, the clergyman would have to be removed to the infirmary. But Caleb Wright was oblivious to consequences, and he continued, earnestly,—

" Contemplation is to us a lost art. It has vanished in the shifting of ideas engendered by the rapid whirl of existence; but life to our more favored brother is slow, very slow. Again, we are unfitted for contemplation by our surroundings and our affairs; for when in these foci of civilization one has succeeded in centring his faculties upon an idea, something external—the rumble of a wagon, or the ringing of a door-bell—is continually shaking the mind from its theme. Or, if one seeks the solitude, anxieties and worldly care follow to distract him. In my own case, speculation is always disturbed by my family duties and my responsibility for the management of this house; for, Mr. Gibbon, whenever you find things running smoothly and efficiently, as we pride ourselves they have run here, you may be certain that thought and reflection have paid the price. I feel that in the world of the concrete, at least, my mind has wrought a success."

"It has, yes, surely it has," conceded the clergyman, politely; though, if facts must be recorded, he winced internally at the fiction to which his assent was giving the color of truth.

Encouraged by the minister's appreciation, Mr. Wright continued,—

"I was speaking of the distractions to thought incident to our civilization. Now, the Indian escapes them entirely. Our petty solicitude for attire, he is above it. Our harassing ambitions, our lust for wealth, have no hold upon him. He is simply an improvident *protégé* of nature. And such homely cares for the physical as life necessitates, he has wisely relegated to the unreasoning factor, woman, so that he is free for his higher destiny. In the silence of the forest he can think undisturbed; by the purling brooks he can lose himself in revery. In connection with the brooks, you know, Mr. Gibbon, what an absorbing interest fishing has for the Indian. Now, what is so indicative of a musing, meditative soul as a love for the piscatorial? I tell you, my friend, the day is coming when that glorious race shall turn from the trout and the salmon, the homely food of the flesh, and shall drag the deep sea of abstraction, bringing up mental food for nations yet unborn."

He paused, perhaps for the due effect of the climax, but

6

Mr. Gibbon did not speak. Possibly he had learned the scientific purport of silence, and was himself angling in the depths. Caleb had really only entered upon his theme, but perverse Chance, who dashes from our lips the cup of pleasure when we have had but one enticing sip, raised her mischievous hand now in the person of the minister's wife, who came with soft apology to announce a caller for her husband. So Caleb Wright was obliged to sit helplessly and behold his audience escaping openly at the door. In a fit of disgust, he sauntered out and went to carry his gospel message to the gardener.

CHAPTER XI.

"I don't know what to do about young Brong," said the banker, to Mr. Todd, as they walked down to business one morning. "I thought he was picking up a little before the folks at the house left, but since Miss Jean has been away—let me see, it's close upon two months now, isn't it?—he's been sinking lower than ever. I've been managing with makeshifts and doing the work myself to give him a chance to straighten out, for he's worth a half-dozen ordinary men to me."

"I had hoped he'd get accustomed to his disappointment in time," said the druggist; "but he doesn't seem to."

"Occasionally he stiffens up and takes hold with something of his old grip, but I notice he always goes off on a worse spree afterwards. I owe Miss Jean a private grudge for the loss of that fellow. Even if he doesn't drink himself to death (which he's most likely to do), he's spoiled as a successful business man; for his mind is unhinged. I don't see but I've got to let him go and take an assistant in his place."

When Frederick Rand reached the bank, Allan Brong was not at his desk. He was needed to-day in reference to some securities, so the banker sent a messenger to his house; but Allan was not at home, nor was he in the town. The young man was sobering off from his last attack, and the banker feared he might have reached that pass beyond which a distracted mind is not to be trusted.

No clue to his whereabouts was to be had. The fourth day after, however, Allan was again at his post. As he volunteered no explanation, his indulgent master required none; still he wondered. Allan could not have followed Jean; that was a trip of ten days at least. Where had he been? Somewhere, and somewhere amid influences, for he had undergone a change; and the banker was overjoyed to find, as the days went by, a change for the better.

He was no longer overcome by those spells of frenzy when he rushed away to stifle his thoughts in liquor. Indeed, from that time, not a drop was known to pass his lips. The restless fever had died out, and a dull lethargy succeeded it; but he had aged in those four days as not in the months of his dissipation. He was quiet, sober, respectable, now, but the hopelessness in his face told that life was henceforth only a lapse of time.

" Brong has got back," the banker announced, at lunch the day of the young fellow's return. " You'd better mention it incidentally in the *Journal*, Price, for people were beginning to get worked up about his disappearance."

" What's he got to say for himself? Where's he been ?" asked the editor.

" Well, he didn't say exactly. I wouldn't make any formal notice of the matter, but just throw in a remark casually that he's turned up all right."

" I wish I could announce the return of our own exiles as well," said the editor. " They've been an unconscionable time gone. When do you look for them? Mr. Wright?"

" Well, pretty soon now, pretty soon; they'll be along shortly. Mrs. Wright is quite well, and Jean is bearing up, —that is, Margaret is bearing up,—I mean, they are both quite well,—that is—Mr. Gibbon, the indifference of the American people to the mission of the Indian will drive me to insanity yet. Here, now, is a new training-school proposed for somewhere down in the valley,—a training-school to corrupt the natives. Mr. Price, if you have the good of mankind at heart, and I believe you have, throw the weight of the *Journal* against this monstrous wrong. Blow one blast of warning against the noxious fumes of education that would torpify the Indian intellect and—and——"

While the gentlemen were listening to the appeal of Caleb Wright, the house-keeper was remarking to the druggist's wife, in a very knowing tone,—

" You remember, Mrs. Todd, once before, four years ago, Mrs. Wright was called to San Francisco."

It was a very simple remark, but Mrs. Todd glanced at Mrs. Gibbon, and Mrs. Gibbon at Mrs. Price, and Mrs. Price back at the house-keeper; and out of that mysterious exchange of women's glances arose a smile, that was mysterious both for its intelligence and surprise.

After that there were no more inquiries after Mrs. Wright's health, but long sessions were held by the ladies whereat interjections seemed to be the popular part of

e 6*

speech. When, therefore, a few weeks later, a carriage drove up to the door, and the household was summoned to the parlor, they were not altogether unprepared to find seated in smiling state Mrs. Wright, and by her side a nurse, holding the new-born heir to the name and traditions of the family. There were reproaches and banter at first by way of greeting, then, on all sides, rejoicing and feasting, calls and congratulations. Caleb Wright alone seemed wanting in appreciation of the new honor that had been vouchsafed him, which was the more singular in view of his regrets over his first-born. A successor in the line of philosophers had proved more welcome in theory than in fact. Perhaps the boy was too close a picture of the Fennimore branch to flatter his vanity; for that erratic ancestor had come again in Margaret's child, and left Jean's fateful combination of hair and eyes.

"By the way, Brong," observed the genial banker, the next evening, as his assistant was preparing to depart, "you must cheer up now. The folks have got back, and what do you think they have brought up by way of surprise? Master Arthur Edgar Wright, a young son."

Frederick Rand had expected to see the young man inspirited by the news, but, instead, Allan Brong clasped his hands tightly about his head, and reeled against the counter. The banker stepped forward, but, without noticing his presence, the young man turned and rushed through the door into the street.

All through the early hours of that night, as Jean Fennimore sat by her open window, she caught the sound of a voice calling, brokenly, " Jean! Jean!" She knew the tones; she knew their meaning; but she did not stir.

It was after midnight when the sound of his voice died away, and suddenly she was startled by the quick, sharp clang of the fire-bell. The town started from sleep. A second alarm, and a third! People half-clad broke out of the houses; the volunteer brigade rushed to the station-house, attached the horses, manned the engine, and went dashing down the street. The fire was somewhere on the outskirts. As they flew along, the vivid, leaping flames conveyed to the encircling woods were outlined against the darkness, growing momently higher and fiercer.

Their coming was taking time, the fire was making ominous head, and they saw as they drew closer that the house was doomed. They slackened speed at the corner, for their haste was useless. But—a glance,—then with a quick thrill of determination they faced the horses to the hill and urged them up the ascent. " Brong's house." The horses were plunging forward under the lash. " Allan Brong's home!" Not one of those young volunteers but knew the story of his sorrow and the history of that house. As the engines drew up before it, suddenly out upon the night broke a cry of mortal anguish. Every man stood rooted, every cheek blanched. Allan Brong—that voice was his, and it came from the depths of the flames!

There was a moment of petrified silence, of breathless, frozen horror; then with one impulse they leaped to the rescue,—a dozen desperate men plunging through the furnace of fire and smiting against windows and doors. The roof tottered overhead, and the walls were seen to sway; still one brave soul pushed on, and forced his way within. But he sprang hurriedly back amid the crash of the falling timbers. Rescue was impossible; the man's fate was upon him: they stood mute and in grim helplessness looked on, till the pitiless flames had left but a black, charred ruin before them.

They did not speak, the catastrophe was too awful. The sorrow and the suffering were done,—they told it in broken tones that night,—poor Allan Brong had ended them in suicide.

CHAPTER XII.

Up in Central Idaho, along the Salmon River, the prospectors had swept like a tidal wave over the country. Where
before the coyote and the Nez Percés had held united possession, now the miner was pushing his adventurous way to
drain the gold from the shining streams. Hardy specimens
of manhood, these, from everywhere and from nowhere;
coming some by stage, some on horseback, more afoot over
the mountains, all ardent with the one design, an open pil-
lage of nature's treasury. Almost at a word claims were
staked, dams thrown up, sluices built, and the men had settled to work as systematically as though they had lived from
infancy upon the spot. Bold, independent souls they were;
men whom no alembic could distil to the ideal,—untaught,
unclean, coarse, repellent, but withal so endowed in the
physical, and in the physical elements of the moral, that one
found himself by an inductive sympathy dropping his traditions, abandoning his taste, and accepting in defiance the
new type of hero.

This tyranny of the senses—how it rules us! When the
skilled scalpel of the artist has cut away the flesh and laid
bare the working of that sublimated thing he calls a soul, we
admire, we embrace. But fold back the living tissue, show
us the man; the earthiness of the medium holds our sight,

and the hero has vanished. Perchance in that other state, when disembodied, etherialized, in the nakedness of souls, we shall stand forth, these flickering purposes of good quenched by our weak distrust, these larger aims crushed under life's homely needs, shall be known and judged; our ideal shall throw back the curtain of our real, and in the grand unveiling we shall all be heroes.

Outlaws were there, desperadoes in plenty, honest men, pure men, villains, every kind but one,—there were no cowards. A weak or cowardly nature could not exist amid these forces; a prerequisite of even life was courage. No conventionality, no social despotism set their price upon hypocrisy, or warped character to their own distorted mould. No fretting plane was forever shaving off the salient angles; no formal force of custom was conscience or dictator. They met on their common attributes, but each man held aloft his sacred personality. Constantly into their midst some stranger drifted with the polish and infirmity of refined life; but the result was always the same: either he quickly abandoned the uncongenial soil, or the soil drew from him the uncongenial dross of civilization.

Along the Salmon River, like an immense flock of birds, the miners had lighted, their weather-worn tents resting down upon the earth like folded wings. The main stream was occupied and apportioned, then the branches and sub-branches, and still the latest comers were pushing on farther and farther towards the sources of the river.

The uppermost settlement, "Last Camp," was located on

one of the final ramifications of the Salmon, a little creek flowing here between hedging willows and cotton-woods. It was a slender little thread of water, but so clear and cold one knew it must have lain in crystal sleep upon the polar heights of the Bitter Root. Now it gave over its sport of somersaults from the rocks and fantastic dances down the dun ravines, and grew alert and defensive, as if fearful of this strange creature it had suddenly come upon who was putting it to such uncanny uses. It leaped in startled awe across the suspicious sluices, then hurried down to join the other brooks, that their united presence might lend it courage to hazard its further progress amid the questionable surroundings.

Last Camp was but a small settlement,—forty-odd men driven to the extremity,—some because they were late arrivals and the nearer ground was all appropriated; others because their former claims had proved unpaying and they were forced to seek new ones; still others because of that peculiarity of organism which impels some to the confines. One meets these characters constantly in the West,—men fleeing from civilization, forever the vanguard of an exodus, who cannot breathe in the crowded mart, but crave the roominess of the frontier.

Such an one was here, the leader of "Last Camp." Jap Lirey might have belonged to the age of myths, he was of such huge proportions. He was predestined to an epic life in his very mould, and the inspiration to such a life was supreme in his environment. No drowsy pastoral could

drone along his days; his ponderous fibres could echo to no
lyric strains. These monster crags that stood like transfixed
warriors, these mute witnesses of a forgotten tragedy—his
heart beat to their hushed pean.

He stood taller by a head than any man about him, and
one often wondered if this instinct of perpetual migration
was not an Ariadne's thread nature had given to lead him
back to his race of giants. As he stood now in the shallow
stream, leaning upon his shovel, bare to the waist, his great
bushy head uncovered (for he scorned the shelter of a hat),
his heavy beard falling upon his hairy breast, he might well
have passed for some god fallen from his high estate and
doomed to the toil of a mortal.

He did his work with easy composure, the strong muscles of his arms scarcely drawn, and one caught himself
measuring the immense power that was latent in that brawn,
and wondering what it might achieve if put to the fullest
tension. Constantly in his work he paused (the habit grew
perhaps out of the necessity of waiting for his partner to
catch up) and, standing erect, surveyed the distant country.
The nearer landscape he overleaped without a glance,—that
was within the range of all; but this border-land which his
great height like an eminence disclosed,—that was his own.
He could stand anywhere and call up a world encircling but
invisible to those beside him.

Was he thinking of the lost race as he stood gazing away
into his expanded horizon? Was he watching for some
beacon to point the uncertain way? There was nothing of

the dreamer about Jap. He had never heard of the old gods; he did not believe in giants; and, if he had strayed from a foreign home, he had swum the river of forgetfulness.

Above on the bank, prying it down with an iron bar, stood Jap's partner, Unco Ben. He was a wiry-bodied, active-brained fellow, who might have risen to eminence in the world of affairs or of politics, but who was somewhat out of place in the mines. He had a habit—most exasperating to the burly Jap—of sitting down deliberately whenever there was a hard piece of work before him and planning out the easiest method of performing it.

"Ye waste double th' time a thinkin' that ye'd hev it done in," Jap was wont to protest; but the man of ideas was not to be repressed, and his partner was forced to allow that Unco's scheming did save him labor, however much of added time it might consume.

Unco Ben's mind was, in truth, so much beyond his own need, in a calling so largely mechanical, that it got, as it were, distributed around to supply the need of those less favored.

The winter before (when as yet Last Camp was unfounded), at the settlement below, the miners found themselves cut off by one of those dreadful avalanches that sometimes isolate sections for months together. The pack-train could not reach them, the provisions gave out, and the men settled down to the conviction that starvation was inevitable. Then it was that the dispirited miners looked in the face of their giant Jap, there, as here, their leader, their chief of men, and found a hopelessness as stolid as their own. Against such a foe his strength could avail nothing; indeed, it made him but more helplessly the victim. But this small, spare man, sitting by the fire and thinking; this scheming mind,—who could tell what it might not evolve? In Unco Ben they set what faint, frail hope they could command, and sat furtively watching the bent figure and waiting,—waiting, watching; watching and waiting. And when at last the small man straightened up, raised his head, and with his quick, keen eye glanced around into the grim faces, swift as an electric spark shot through those silent men the knowledge that he had won, and shouts—wild, frenzied shouts—tore through the air; and the man had never spoken a word.

Yet much as they owed to Unco Ben, deep as was the gratitude freely accorded, their hearts did not cleave to him as through that dire winter it had come to cleave to one whose service was perhaps slight by comparison. A lawless autocrat is the human heart; reason and judgment may coerce, but by some subtle law it yields its incense only when the fibres of feeling are touched. And their affection had been filched from them by another,—Luke,—"Larfin' Luke" they christened him through that time in impatient derision,"—but the tone of utterance had softened since, and was now as near an epithet of endearment as these hard men could venture.

He was treated by all with a rough familiarity which was

but their awkward way of indicating their attachment. If a ballot had been taken, who was the last man they would have seen set his back to the camp and strike out for the "world" again, that man would have been, by the vote of every miner, Luke.

He was a sunny-natured fellow, a shuffling, limp, ungainly creature, whose arms and legs seemed always inclined to dally along behind the rest of his person, an open-faced man, full of generous impulses. One felt in looking at him that somewhere in his length of days the light of happiness had pierced and flooded all his being. From the humble home of his childhood, perhaps, a glowing beam had shot athwart the world, whose twilight was still radiance in the gloom of that stricken camp.

Through the long, leaden silence, when men spoke low in the presence of approaching as of a present death, Larfin' Luke spun his yarns and cracked his jokes in a very abandon of mirth. True, the face was haggard and the laugh was hard, and they all knew it was but a poor, weak effort to distract their thoughts. It angered them—this " everlastin' chatterin'," for they were hungry and irritable; but they caught themselves listening involuntarily, and sometimes in self-forgetfulness a smile flickered across their ashen lips, and he was satisfied. So it was that Luke had won his name, and so it was he won the simple hearts of the miners.

All this was back in the old camp. They had abandoned it in the spring, and come up to try the ground here in Ramrod Gulch. Into Last Camp had drifted several from other parts of the fields, and some outsiders who had come too late for the nearer available diggings. Of the latter, one had entered the claim adjoining Larfin' Luke's, and in course of time, close at hand two cabins were standing on the hill-side.

In a new camp as in a new country, cabin-room is scarce, and each man is held entitled to " enough to stretch in" and no more. It was against the new-comer, therefore, that while in Luke's cabin the bunks lined every side of the wall, in his there was but one. He had no partner on the claim, no lodger in the cabin. Unsociability is the unpardonable sin, and this man committed it daily.

He was guilty of another equally offensive breach of border breeding, for, though he rallied with the others at the Crater, he did not join the drinking. A severe stricture this upon the honest custom of his fellows, and one which insured him their cordial dislike. Occasionally he redeemed himself a little by the recklessness of his gambling, but he always lost; and what they conceded in good-will for conformity, they took back in contempt for failure.

As the months followed each other, they began to notice that a fatality attended this man. Every ill-luck that befell the camp passed the others over and lit upon him. Twice, on the eve of a clean-up, a thief slipped in and made away with his dust; then the dam broke just above his claim and swept the gold broadcast over the bed of the creek; and later, in the fall, while prying it down, the bank had caved, and the man in falling had struck across his iron bar and dislocated his shoulder. It was after a succession of such mishaps that he came to be looked upon by the miners as fated to misfortune, so his own name was discarded for one more apposite, and they called him henceforth " Onlucky."

While Onlucky, owing to the accident, was confined to his bunk, his sins of commission and omission were temporarily overlooked, and, with a serviceable charity that did them credit, the miners took turns in watching at his bedside. But the most welcome presence was ever Larfin' Luke, whose loud, cheery voice seemed at the threshold to summon other spirits as jovial as himself.

They grew to be, in a measure, friends, Luke and Onlucky; and through their long night vigils together, Luke became gradually aware that a sorrow dogged this man's life as persistently as did ill-fortune. It was a vague story, about a son whom he had loved and lost,—that was all Luke could glean of it,—but, as the story passed among the miners, it explained and excused to them much of Onlucky's eccentricity. Many of these men—some ruffianly, some honest,—were carrying deep in their own hearts the memory of a tragic past, and each in his own way was stifling its echoing voices.

In the presence of this knowledge they interpreted Onlucky anew. His fitful moods, when in sullen despondency he isolated himself, or in reckless eagerness sought the gaming table and staked his last ounce of dust only to lose —they understood them now, in the light of that dimly-outlined story, of which, with a chivalric sense of honor, they never sought a further knowledge.

7*

As Onlucky became convalescent and their attentions were no longer needed, the miners gradually withdrew again, but henceforth in their thoughts of him there was no animosity. Often still of an evening, Luke would drop in to retail the news and the gossip to the lonely man. In one of these chance visits, he informed Onlucky that " they'd been havin' a hell uv a time in th' bottoms." " Mahog'ny" had come up from the settlement below, and already in three days there had been five knock-down fights and a murder in her section. The miners were thinking of " firin' her out," Luke said, " right at the start, an' savin' wus trouble, for she war the allfiredest devil in the hull gold-fields."

But the autumn crept into winter, and winter into spring, and down in Hell's Half-Acre Mahog'ny still lingered, and the brawls and the riots were unsuppressed.

CHAPTER XIII.

MINERS are to the general mind a class whose chief attributes are recklessness and prodigality; and mining an occupation that possesses all the unhallowed allurement of exceptional profit and questionable repute. It may reconcile the consciences of some to know that the work of placer mining is scarcely more adventurous or eventful than plowing, and that the genus miner has as many distinct species as the animal kingdom.

Work in the large quartz-mines, with the necessary divisions of labor, partakes of the conditions of work in factories or any similar establishments; but work on the placers is quite another thing. If a stranger had passed along down Ramrod Gulch, he would have seen at intervals of several hundred feet a few men, generally two, sometimes one, now on the slope, now in the stream, engaged in the simple occupation of prying off the bank, or (standing in great gum boots) of shovelling up the stones from the river bed. Little halo of romance here, but plenty of dull, monotonous toil; and as for the fabulous profit,—well, they hadn't seen much of it, these men in Ramrod, certainly not enough to lend any unsanctified aspect to their calling. Barring the sessions at the Crater, they led an isolated, eventless life, and their occasional wild orgies seemed all that kept them from fossilizing.

79

In the spring of the next year, however, the camps on the Salmon River suffered no dearth of excitement, for rumors began to be active of a threatened Indian outbreak. The North-west was as yet a country too new to be under a system of reservations, though a few years later the attempt was made to transfer these Indians to Northern Montana. Then Central Idaho became historical as the scene of General Howard's movements against Chief Joseph, who at the Big Hole surprised and almost annihilated Gibbon's force. It was in the heart of this Nez Percés country that the hardy miners were pushing their fortunes, and the Indians were disposed to resent the invasion of their rights and their territories.

At this early time throughout the Central West the Mormon church was a power mysterious, jealous, elusive, successful,—a power dreaded doubly in that its malign creed left no principle of justice or equity to guide its dealings with the Gentile. The nations were a spoil and a prey for Zion, and any license was legitimate that increased her power. The country was still shuddering over the horror of the Mountain Meadow massacre, and the West felt helpless before a foe who masked his hatred and found in the disguise of a savage the safeguard for his treachery.

When, therefore, it was whispered that back of the present discontent was church ambition, and that the leaders of the outbreak were renegade Mormons, the miners knew that subtlety and craft would not be lacking in the councils. The larger camps and more thickly populated sections were secure, for their numbers precluded all idea of an attack. It was the outlying districts, the detached settlements that felt the danger; for upon them the hostiles could swoop down, massacre, and escape again to their mountain fastnesses. Fifteen of the forty-five men from Last Camp shouldered their picks and rifles and retired from the outpost. Here in the gate-way of the gold-fields other men might stand and break the shock if they saw fit; for themselves, they preferred to join the majority.

But the alarm to this northern border proved gratuitous, for, in their wonted perversity of design, the allies circled to the southward, and fell instead upon a body of prospectors, who, trusting to the security of distance, had ventured out beyond the reach of help. Several of these unwary bands, some ignorant, some foolhardy, were in turn surprised and cut off. Parties were sent out for pursuit and retribution, but the enemy managed generally to evade them and secure his retreat. All through the summer, report followed report of depredations and barbarities, but the fever of money-getting still postponed an organized, persistent effort at suppression.

Now, however, summer had gone, the fall was passing, and the Indians were moving north again to retire into winter quarters. The miners breathed freely, for the season's raids were over. But the leaders, as it proved, had projected another diversion before withdrawing, one that they trusted might leave an assurance of their faithful antagonism as well as a wholesome memory of their prowess. It was on a crisp

f

autumn morning that a man came dashing into Last Camp
with the news that the "Reds" were coming, and, as fifteen
had retired, only thirty men were left to face the fight.

There was a hurrying of feet in that early dawn, but every
step rang firm; a quick rallying of men down by the Crater,
but every face was resolute. They sent the messenger on to
ride his fleetest for help, then they set to work making ready
for the fight. Boulders were rolled down, the loose stones
stacked, and such barricades and defences as time and their
meagre material permitted were hastily thrown together, for
they knew well the nature of the attack they must sustain.

Foremost in the work, straining now those powerful arms
till every muscle was like an iron rod, stood the giant Jap
Here was a call for strength, and he gave it without stint.
He seemed to be tearing out the very mountain-side and
heaving it in front of the camp. Every few minutes he
stood erect, shaded his eyes, and peered away. Now by
chance he glanced up, and, suddenly pointing off in the
distance, " What's thet ?"

There beyond the valley, high up on the other slope of
the mountain, a man was moving slowly, stooping every few
minutes to pick something from the ground. Who could
it be? What was he doing off there in the early dawn?
Every one stood still watching the moving figure unconscious
of its peril. At last, in a dazed whisper, "It's Onlucky,"
said Luke; "it's thet damned Onlucky. I heered him pass
the trail afore the house more'n an hour ago. He's wanderin'
in his head ag'in."

As he spoke, Unco Ben, with quicker wit than the rest, raised his rifle and fired. The fated man did not even turn. Another shot, but the distant figure was climbing higher and higher up the steep. There was a pause; once again Jap swept his eyes over the range of the horizon; then, saying, simply, " I'll fetch him," he strode out across the valley.

Breathlessly the miners' gaze followed their leader as with quick, long strides he crossed the plain. Had it ever been so far—that ridge? Had Jap ever walked so slowly? Surely he was scarcely moving; and all that ground to cover! He would never do it, never. Yet yes, he had struck the slope, and Onlucky had caught sight of him; but he did not move, only stood listlessly waiting the other's ascent. The men were together now, and—why were they parleying? why were they delaying? They saw Jap stretch out his mighty hand and, seizing Onlucky by the arm, drag him down the mountain, and on across the plain, over the creek, and back into the camp; and when the two came close, the miners beheld tightly clasped in Onlucky's hand a great bunch of wild flowers, and they whispered to each other that he had lost his mind.

They felt it more certainly when, while Onlucky returned with Larfin' Luke to his cabin for rifle and ammunition, Jap related the events of the meeting.

" Thar he stud," said Jap, " es stupid an' onconsarned es ef I hadn't most knocked my wind out climbin' up that mounting; an' when I ast him what he war doin' foolin' round thar on the top, he sez, kind uv happy like, 'It's my son's birthday ter-day, an' I'm a celebratin',—my son what's lost.' I war all struck in a lump. I 'most forgot ter tell him the Reds were on us, an', when I did tell him, he jest looked about indifferent, es ef thet didn't consarn him anny, an' sed he couldn't come yet a bit till he'd got more posies, —an' the Nez Percés waitin' ter chaw us up! I jest tuk him by the arm an' packed him down out uv thet without no more chinnin', I kin tell yer."

And shortly after he finished, Luke came up and observed that "ef that Onlucky warn't the clean daftest man loose," might he die with his boots on, for he'd "got his cabin all dec'rated with branches uv trees an' sech like, till it looked like a fir-wood, an'——"

What he might have revealed further was never known, for without a sound of warning the bullets came whistling down the wind, and they knew the Nez Percés were here, and that every rock and stump and tree concealed a man.

The miners dipped quickly behind the barricade, and returned the shot, and so for more than an hour each side kept up a desultory fire, picking off the men as by any cause they became exposed. The attack had expected to find the miners unprepared, and in the reception the surprise was clearly greatest to themselves.

Three of the leaders were seen to retire to the rear, and the miners might have been enlightened as well as advised could they have heard, uttered in good, hard English,—

"How in thunder did the devils get the scent of us? We'll never stomp them out behind them rocks. They'll be havin' help too in no time, and then the game's up. Go, Jeffrey, take a squad, sneak back along the chapparel, and wait. We'll try to draw 'em from cover, and if they take the bait, beat up against the flank, and double on 'em. There's no time to lose. We must set the red dogs on before the recruits get here."

The miners could not infer a double design; they were, besides, too few in number to guard all the approaches. They had seen the consultation, they inferred its decision when, at a signal, with little united method but a fierce individual purpose, the allies broke from their shelter and bore down upon the camp. But thirty determined men were standing like a wall of stone against the shock. As the charging force came within easy range, Jap's slow voice called the order, and together the rifle-balls sped home, true to the aim of the marksmen. They stood erect now, the miners, and poured their shot without a break into the advancing lines. No Nez Percés force would stand in the face of that steady death,—such was not their theory of fighting. They quickly divided and sought again the protection of the nearer rocks and trees, and the attack was turned into sharp-shooting once more.

The stratagem had failed, but the miners in their own extremity furnished the fatal chance the leaders had sought. The little band had made good use of their lead,—the path of the advance attested that; but the deadly aim of the

8

marksmen was making havoc among their numbers as well. Every few minutes some one was borne to the rear, killed or disabled, and turned over to the charge of the one nurse, Mahog'ny.

Jap glanced over the thinning line of his comrades, and felt that some way an end must be put to this murderous fire. He must venture a sortie, for the assailants once driven back and scattered would not form again, but would make for their ponies and ride off.

He turned to give the word, and there, staggering to the rear, with the blood trickling in a bright stream from his breast, down his blue flannel shirt and along his gum boot, was Luke,—Luke, the idol of the camp. He laughed in his leader's face,—this untaught, grimy hero,—the same brave, broken laugh that had mocked the silence when they two had starved together; and the sound of that voice roused Jap to fury. With the strength of a Titan he tore a path through the barricade, and, leaping over, called the men to follow. They followed, indeed,—all but one; for close at the head, side by side with Jap in that charge, marched Onlucky, the deadliest fighter of them all that day.

The darkened faculties had cleared now, the "daftness" had gone with the dawn; and the luckless man, calm, sagacious, was marching in front of his fellows, fighting not recklessly, but well. While the burly Jap loaded and fired continuously, the other deliberately levelled his rifle, but every ball brought down a foe. Jap's body, too, was a very target for the enemy. He was covered with wounds, and his whole person was bathed in blood, while Onlucky had escaped untouched.

The enemy had fallen steadily back before the miners' advance, but, now, in place of scattering, they seemed preparing for a counter-charge. What did it mean? Jap pressed impetuously forward; but instantly Onlucky turned, his alert mind to-day scenting every danger. There, creeping down upon them beyond the flank, was a new force of men; soon the miners must be surrounded and cut off. With a quick cry of "Halt!" he pointed down, and then, in the mouth of that terrible wedge, Onlucky massed his men and began the retreat to the barricade. It was a task that taxed his utmost skill and his nicest judgment, for those in front bore down with a yell, and those on the flank, seeing the retiring movement, broke and ran pell-mell for the enclosure.

Far to the front, in a hand-to-hand encounter, wielding his massive arms like flails about him, Jap was backing his way, interposing his huge body like a rampart between the onslaught and his retreating countrymen. But the tall form was seen to sway a moment in the air, then the upraised arm dropped forceless, the uncovered head sank, and slowly, lingeringly, the man settled down in his tracks.

A voiceless despair fell upon the hearts of the little band, but their faces were grim and unflinching; for it was fight to the death, and no quarter with this foeman.

The men on the flank were near to the enclosure, and, knowing that there lay the last hope of making a stand,

Onlucky gave the word, and the miners, too, went rushing for the camp. They reached it almost together, the one breaking in from the side, the other from the front, and here within the barricade, against the fearful odds, each man stood up to battle for his life. But hark! a shot!— a shot!—another and another! An instant they paused, listened, glanced out; then, with a cry of baffled rage, the assailants turned and broke from the place. There was a flying of feet off towards the willow thicket, and the next minute a band of mounted warriors was dashing across the valley taking the trail into the mountains.

The rescuing party rode in. They had come with speed, but none too soon to save the remnant of the camp. When the little body gathered together to sum up the results of the fight, it was a sad record they had to show. Of the thirty men that stood together at the dawn, nine only answered "Living," to their names, and, of the nine, five only had escaped unhurt.

But Luke—Larfin' Luke—why did he not answer? And Mahog'ny—where was Mahog'ny? The faces that had looked stoically down the muzzles of the levelled guns were averted now. Dead? Death were a benediction. And when they went to bring in the body of their leader, Jap, he, too, was missing; not dead, alas! not dead,—gone to the mercy of the savage and the "saint."

Ah! you who sit nestling in the arms of civilization, whose tender flesh shrinks from the coarse contact of clay, do you know at what cost was purchased the ease that enfolds you?

Ask these—these common men, these large-boned, hard-grained, coarse, unselfish men, whose voices jar upon the sensitive ear, whose unlettered speech affronts the taste, whose very presence is an offence to the civilization they fought and died for. No minstrel sings the valor of the pioneer. His deeds are left to their ignoble setting, and his sons in the land he ransomed pass him by for a daintier hero with nicer accent and no earth-stains on his hands. "Mere animal courage theirs!" Oh, the nice discernment of the unvulgared taste! Is there an attribute of the spiritual that is not rooted in the animal; or a fibre of the animal that is not instinct with the spirit? Will you grant a heavenly grace to the figure yonder in trimmest broadcloth pouring forth in studied eloquence his " Love your neighbor as yourself," and deny it to these half-clad, generous souls who, loving their neighbor far beyond themselves, fell at the perilous portals of progress? Ah, in that imperishable record where the grossness of the physical has no sway, they are known for what they are! He has set their names close beside His own, for they, like Him, have laid down their lives for their friends.

8*

CHAPTER XIV.

THE calamity that had overtaken Jap, Luke, and the woman cast over the camp a gloom far beyond that of the death of their comrades. Death is a finality, and in its sorrow there is still, amid such scenes as this, a consolation; but the fate of those three,—Onlucky rose from his seat before the Crater, walked out to the corral behind the camp, and saddled a horse. He led it up in front of the saloon, before the assembled men, and waited. They understood it, this silent call for volunteers, but it seemed such a senseless, foolhardy venture. The relief corps had come to fight, but they had not come to ride into a nest of savages for a sentiment, and they kept their seats. They had not known Jap, —brave, unselfish Jap; they had not known Luke,—Larfin' Luke; but slowly, one after another, the four unwounded men of Last Camp rose, passed out to the corral, saddled, and came back.

Unco Ben on his one available leg hobbled in to the bar, and, bringing a bottle, handed it to Onlucky. He drew a long, deep draught and passed it to his neighbor, who did the same; the fifth man drained the bottle and returned it to Ben. Then they mounted, wheeled about, struck spurs, and went riding across the plain.

It was a simple matter following the trail, and they rode

in single file silently. There was little call for speech, and they were too painfully engrossed with the events of the day to incline much to conversation. Constantly there loomed up in their minds a sense of the hopelessness of their errand, but they thrust the thought aside and followed on. It was the blind leading of a desire to convince themselves that no chance remained for these lost comrades.

The country they were traversing was wild and broken. They had left behind them in the valley the tufted sward, the scattered groves, and had come out upon the rocky foot-hills that swelled into the Bitter Root. These were covered with thick sage-brush whose ashen foliage looked tawny where the purple shade slanted across it, for the sky was moody and sullen to-day. It had been meditating rain all morning; now in the early afternoon it seemed to have definitely decided upon it, but the drops still lingered, though the clouds lay with lowering brows upon the very ridges of the mountains. The peaks were towering in their white splendor against the malign heavens, and a nimbus swath stretched like a forbidding hand across the gap and gave to the frowning cliffs a threatening mien as the men plunged between them into the narrow cañon. Their hoof-beats echoed and re-echoed against the granite walls, till it seemed as though a thousand horse were leaping down the rocks and clattering on behind. The strataed piles leaned over in dull amazement at the noise, and a silvery cascade laughed in derision as they passed.

Soon they were beyond the gorge, out upon the open trail

that wound among the mountains. They had followed it but a short distance when they halted abruptly. Here the band had divided; the smaller part taking the upper, the larger, the lower road. After a debate, the little party decided to keep along the latter as being the easier of ascent, and so a more likely way for the wounded and the prisoners.

For three hours longer they rode along, following the trail through the labyrinths of the hills; then they drew rein and consulted again. It was unlikely that the enemy, knowing a pursuit to be impossible, would go far before camping with their wounded. It became evident to the miners that they had taken the wrong path, and nothing remained but to wheel about and ride back over their course.

It was quite dark when they reached the divide, but without pausing they struck into the other trail and hurried on. The moon was at its full. It tore a rent in the clouds and peered down a moment, but it had no interest in these five silent horsemen, so it withdrew again.

The miners had gone scarcely two miles when, looking over the brow of a hill, they saw below in the valley the gleam of a camp-fire. They slackened their pace now, and cautiously, with the stealth of savages themselves, led their horses down to a little knoll that commanded the encampment. They could see it all plainly by the light of the fire; to the right, the painted warriors, stretched upon the ground asleep, and next to them, the wounded, some sitting, some reclining, some shifting from one posture to another in a vain effort at comfort.

On the left side were extended ten men. They wore the garb of their fellows, and seemed to have separated from them for a closer approach to the heat. But as the light flared up, the miners caught the profile of a face and it was white. These, then, were the emissaries of Zion, the saintly leaders of the raid. Their day's work had begotten no uncomfortable twinges, for their attitudes were easy and they slept.

Between the Mormons and their allies, directly in front of the surveying group, and clearly outlined by the brightness, were the prisoners. There was Jap sitting, his huge form erect, his bound hands on his knees; and Luke, extended at full length, for, as less disabled, his feet had been secured as well. Close beside him, her elbow supported against a stone and her head sunk upon her breast, was Mahog'ny, " the all-firedest devil in the gold-fields."

A long look they turned upon the scene—these men,—a look of hopeless farewell to the three. They were beyond all succor. What chance of rescue, with that scout pacing to and fro on ceaseless guard, with those wounded men sitting awake in stolid suffering? None: they had come; they had seen; they faced about to go back. But—look—that last man is dismounting. What is it? They pull their horses up with a jerk, and stare. Yes, there he stands. He has thrown off his hat, and is pulling his belt in tight. He draws out his long knife, and twice runs his hand along its edge. It is keen; he puts it back. Now he steps up, and, from the belts of his two nearest companions, takes the revolvers and sticks them beside his own.

A shudder shoots through the hearts of those four watching men, for well they know now his errand, and the awful purpose of the weapons. Self-destruction is a privilege accorded every one when it is his only escape from the Indian, nor will the popular voice call it by that coward word—suicide. Ah, yes, they know the mission of the weapons; and, sitting there with their fascinated eyes fixed upon the still, calm face of this desperate man, they know, too, with a kind of horror, that he will not fail. They trust him, with a trust that is born not of knowledge, not of reason, but of the soul-power looking from his eyes.

With the trust comes a thought, and with the thought a hope. He took but two weapons; two only must die; he will save one. Every miner leans from the saddle, and, as the man passes, bends close and whispers,—each one the same,—"Save Luke," "Save Luke," "Save Luke, Onlucky," "Save Luke."

Slowly, cautiously under the darkness he steps out; then they see him drop and on his breast crawl down amid the brush. But he turns from his course and circles round, getting to wind of the Mormons. He is alongside now, by the glow of the fire they see him extend himself as in sleep, and slowly, inch by inch, roll his way closer and closer into the camp. The guard turns; the quick ear has caught a sound. Instinctively four rifles are levelled, four triggers cocked; but no, "it is only one of them Mormon hounds." He turns again; he paces back; and now—a spring—a flashing knife, once, twice, a glitter of steel, a backward bound, and—two pistol-shots ring out that echo forever in the ears of those listening men.

In the camp every one is on his feet. Attacked? Surprised? A consternation of silence is on them for a moment; but the cheated guard is standing, pointing to—there are but two prisoners now; the pistols are still smoking in their hands, and they are dead.

So it is a rescue. With a yell of defiance twenty men plunge back to the corral, while, out there in the darkness, with a superhuman strength Onlucky is dashing up the slope, bearing something in his arms. Four mounted men are sitting motionless; four levelled guns are covering his advance. Now he is here; he has not failed; he is here. He rushes to the rear, tosses his burden before him to the saddle, and leaps up. The four men turn, and—he has saved not Luke, not Luke, but the woman!

For a moment there is a hush, then from the lips of the men, these men whom danger has made nearer than brothers, there breaks a low, deep curse, and each, as he strikes spurs and dashes past, leans close to hiss again in Onlucky's ears his awful execration. Ever through that ride,—that terrible ride in the darkness, that terrible ride of death,—shuddering down the wind comes the echo of their curses, for he has saved not Luke but the woman.

And she—that bane of the camp, that enemy of all true men, riding there with only this one brave soul between her and the friends behind—what does she think of those muffled curses, rolling down the din of the hoof-beats like the low, broken mutterings of thunder? She can read **On-lucky's** motive. He was not of her followers; he never came to Hell's Half-Acre; it was not that. But he felt what she had felt in that instant of his appearing beside the camp-fire, that she could not kill herself; with her black, crime-steeped soul she dare not kill herself. So merry Larfin' Luke had died instead.

By the time they have left the valley and struck into the mountain-trail, the Nez Percés are mounted and in hot pursuit. The miners can hear them speeding their ponies, and catch the guttural call of the braves urging them on from the camp. They too are dashing up the padded slope into the granite road. All along that flying file, white and red, every man leans over, gives rein, and drives the spurs into the reeking flanks, till the horses seem like an animated whirlwind tearing down the path.

Onlucky—his name belies him once, for has he not by good chance mounted Jap's horse to-day? It carries its double burden with the high courage of its master, and holds its place, last of the five, not leader now, still close upon the heels of its flying mates.

They are rounding the base of the mountain, tense, straining shadows, with meteor eyes. The mettled hoofs are striking out a double belt of stars along the way, and the night has hushed its breath at the fierce pulsing of feet.

They are dashing along the cañon. The rough-ribbed walls are muttering at their clang; the silvery cascade still laughs derisively; and the troop that followed their cause at noon, traitorwise, has deserted and joined the hostile cavalcade behind.

They are out upon the foot-hills; more than half the ground is covered, and still the miners hold the front, and still Jap's horse rides bravely at their heels. But it is weakening. In their faces the two catch the foam tossed up from its mouth like spray. The steam is rising from its sides, and —it stumbles once, but is caught back, and the spurs are pressing its bloody flanks and urging it mercilessly on.

Another stretch. They are taking the last low swell. Four horses are clattering at a distance, and clear and clearer are striking the hoof-beats of the pursuit. Whiz! a bullet! It has passed right by them. The leader is close behind, but he is shooting at random in the dark.

So near the camp, they can see the blazing fire the miners have built to guide them home. Right into its light four horsemen are riding now, so near! so near! The treacherous moon is peering out, and—another ball! The arm about her drops, for that one has sped home. Onlucky turns; the eyes that meet his gleam with a sinister triumph, and the face, like his own, is white. A moment, and the rescue may be in vain. He rises in his stirrups and puts the muzzle against her temple.

" Yes," she says.

" Yes," she repeats,—and it is done.

There by the fire-light the miners are mounting, and the pursuers with a parting volley have drawn rein. They are moving back now along the rocky trail, and Onlucky is staggering into the camp afoot, with a dead woman in his arms.

CHAPTER XV.

THE next day was spent by the miners at the Crater. There was but one way of burying their emotions and of restoring their repressed spirits, and this was in liquor. Not that it could wash out the painful, lingering thoughts. Those fresh, narrow head-boards there by the bare mounds, —the sun of summer and the storm of winter would beat down, and wear the simple names away; but no heat of sun or stress of storm could wear the memories from the hearts of these rough, true men. Yet the first keen edge of suffering must be blunted, for the dead were at rest, but the living must take up their life of toil again.

Onlucky was there with the rest, his crippled arm in a sling. His reckless mood was on him; he had relapsed into his old self, and he was gambling. Once only, into those feverish, bloodshot eyes came the calm, self-centred look of yesterday. It was along in the afternoon that one of his companions, grown rash under the influence of drink, leaned down over the cards and drawled querulously,—

"Why didn't ye fetch Luke, Onlucky?"

Slowly he raised his head, and, looking full into the eyes of his questioner, drew his revolver from his belt and set it beside him on the table. That was all, but no man took the

98

challenge; and never did the miners solve the mystery of that day.

The Indian raids continued for a time, but Last Camp had established its reputation in arms, and was subjected to no further experiments. Still, security for the country was not established till, some twelve years later, the Nez Percés were ordered to the reservation, and led Miles that chase to the British lines which has become memorable in the annals of border warfare.

The mining excitement continued along the Salmon River for a few years unabated; then it became gradually apparent that the placers were giving out. Rumors were constantly afloat of the discovery of rich quartz-leads, and the presence of the placers was, of course, proof that such existed. A few good claims were struck, and the work of developing commenced, but they were not many. All the men had faith in the reality of rich leads, but quartz-mining was outside their department, and placer-workers are apt to be conservative. So one by one, as the ground was worked out and the boom went down, the men rolled up their blankets and struck out for Montana, Colorado, or yet more distant fields.

The Salmon-River basin was abandoned almost as speedily as it had been occupied; a few detached settlements alone remained of the hundred thousand men who had flocked in to the gold-fields. Idaho was restored to its vast native desolation; and only the torn, scarred valleys kept the memory of the rushing host that had come and gone.

Last Camp was deserted with the rest. But two of its

members still linked destinies with the bleak country. Unco Ben, realizing at last his aptitude for the mercantile, but unable to dissever the bonds of habit, moved down to the nearest quartz-district and opened a general store, part saloon, part supply-dépôt. And Onlucky—he had grown unfit for the society of men. His turbulent soul felt drawn to the deep solitudes of the mighty hills where he could bury himself and relieve his heart in speech.

Before the breaking up of the camp, during one of those fitful moods in which he fled to burn the fever out in solitary vigils, he had mounted his broncho and galloped up along the creek to the lonely shelter of the frozen peaks. On his return he brought with him some samples of rock which he announced as specimens from a wonderful lead he had discovered. The rock did not seem to warrant his enthusiasm. To be sure, there were traces of gold, and it was free-milling, but anywhere along the creek such rock was to be had for the taking. Still, so sanguine was he of his find, that he packed up immediately to take possession ; and several of his fellow-miners, kindled unconsciously by his enthusiasm, saddled and rode along, with the unavowed intention of locating a claim if the glowing report was verified.

But when they reached the spot and beheld Onlucky's lead, they were content to leave him the region undivided. Poor, distracted creature, the last vestige of reason must have forsaken him when he anchored a hope to this forlorn prospect! They besought him to abandon the ledge and strike out with them across the range, but he was obstinate.

The blind, persistent, unreasoning obstinacy that seems to be at the root of a miner's character had him in its fatal sway, and held him to the spot. So the men retired, and there in the heart of the mountains they left Onlucky,—brave, silent, " daft" Onlucky, alone with his barren lead.

What a strange force lurks in human faith! A frail fibre of thought shoots down into the depths of the invisible, and, grasping some deep-lying power, imbibes a foreign vigor that holds the mind high-poised above knowledge or evidence. Here, in a faith invincible, Onlucky struck his pick. About him reigned eternal silence. The mighty forests of the darkling slopes, whether obliterated under the avalanche of snows, or restored in the breath of vernal breezes, were alike distant and mute. No voice of nature came to hint a kinship in a common claim of life; and the voice of man sounded in his ears only when once or twice a season he went down to the settlement for supplies. The low, regretful murmur of the summer wind and the shrill raging of the winter's blasts were all that broke the silence, and the man's fitful spirit was tossed on their every breath.

It was an immense ledge of rock on which Onlucky had pitched for his mine, a ledge that sloped away to the little creek obliquely, and was continued in a similar formation on the other side. Close beside the shaft he built his cabin, and night and morning he could look down the slanting cut and see in fancy the glittering wealth entombed in the rocky hill-side. Year after year, through the winter he labored at the lead, in summer working the placers to supply his simple wants.

It came to him one day that the quickest way, on the whole, to develop his mine would be to tunnel in from the bed of the creek, and hit the lead on its level. Abandoning the upper shaft, patiently he commenced anew at the base of the slope; and henceforth his life centred on the creek,—in summer on the failing placers, for support; in winter on the slowly-gaining tunnel, for—a fortune.

CHAPTER XVI.

THE desertion of the Salmon-River diggings put an end to the artificial prosperity of Portland. The transient populace that had thronged its streets was scattered; most had gone in search of new fields, but many, disappointed of success in the mines, had forsworn the allurements of chance and turned to the surer promise of the Oregon soil. Portland settled back to a calm, wholesome business life. But there was a vast difference between the hamlet which the stampede had found, and the city which it left.

The place was steadily growing, and stretching its elastic borders, and the Fennimore house, which had stood in the immunities of the suburbs, was finding its isolation persistently encroached upon. It might even have been jostled by its invading neighbors did not its stretch of grounds hold them off at a decorous distance.

"I don't see, Jean, but what we will have to move away for the accommodation of the new-comers," remarked Mrs. Wright, ironically, one Sunday afternoon, as her glance swept past the household assembled on the lawn and rested on a half-finished structure hugging the farther side-fence. "I did think the town would stop when it got out here, but this last house completes the circle. We are surrounded, and I suspect we might as well capitulate."

103

"Oh, neighbors don't disturb me," said Jean, composedly. "I should be rather disposed to welcome them if each didn't filch a new section from our landscape. We lost Goat Island to the Richardses, half a mile of the river to the Lees, and here Mt. Adams is appropriated bodily. It is so uncomfortable to awake in the morning and look out upon a familiar scene, only to find its most prominent feature spirited away. Now when I want an unbroken view I am obliged to climb to the top of the ridge back yonder."

"Yes, and even that will be occupied in time," interrupted her sister, disgustedly.

"Not to-day, I hope," said Jean, rising and putting on the hat that had been dangling from her hand. "I was going to stroll up that way, and I shouldn't like to find that an edifice had sprung up in the night and taken possession of my favorite retreat."

"I can't understand the feeling that impels you to those hill-tops every time you can escape."

There was a tincture of resignation in Margaret's tone, as though she had reached the philosophic stage of enduring the incomprehensible in her sister.

"Nor I the feeling that anchors you to this patch of lawn," said Jean, laughing. She drew on her glove leisurely, and stepped across the walk to the inviting grass.

"Thurgar! take Thurgar," called a sturdy little fellow from the piazza. She extended her hand, and Arthur Edgar, or "Thurgar," as the struggling tongue of childhood had contracted it, ran eagerly across and put his own little pudgy one within it.

"Will you take the rest of us, for the same pleading, Miss Jean?" asked Frederick Rand, as they passed the wicker settee on which he was lounging and enjoying his cigar.

"If the rest of us have the same desire to go," she answered.

Whereupon the banker left his comfortable seat, threw away his cigar, picked up his cane, and sauntered along beside her.

"I think it is time some one was contesting Master Thurgar's prerogatives," he drawled, in excuse for his coming. "This monopoly of his aunt's attention will make somebody jealous one of these days."

"Jealousy of Thurgar is an unlicensed emotion," said his aunt, in pointed pleasantry. "Children have an incontestable right to love."

"It is not his right to love, but his right to exclusive love, Miss Jean. He ought to share with his elders."

"His elders have neither his need nor his——" She hesitated, then added, defiantly, "nor his worth."

Frederick Rand beamed upon her with ingenuous reproach.

"How severe you are! You rate us men, I fear, very low in your scale of values."

"I rate men! Deliver me from such an occupation."

"You surely do not advocate the old hermit theories of life," he said, a little aggressively. "Ah, Miss Jean, the earth is so clayey it wouldn't do for men to be too spiritual.

If we were the saints we might be, there would be danger of premature translation."

" We have no call for undue alarm, I trust. I had thought it might be some time before men's wings would provoke a very perilous flight."

Frederick Rand laughed quietly. Her cynicism was, to the banker, this woman's unique charm. Other men had other tastes, yet many seemed to find in Jean Fennimore the specific quality he most fancied. Perchance her beauty was a glamorous medium through which each could see what he was predisposed to seeing, for Jean was very beautiful. Her figure had developed the rounded fulness it lacked in earlier days, but the old fragility still lurked in a certain litheness which preserved the pliancy of girlhood in the ripe grace of the woman.

The airy merriment had given place to an expression a trifle over-sad at times, but habitually calm and self-contained. It was a pleasure to the worldly man to see a woman who never forgot herself; who could be composed without being reserved; who received her acquaintances cordially, even gratefully, yet held her isolation inviolate. There was a fascination in her unconscious aloofness, and the banker was willing she should make herself a little pedestal, seeing how she graced it.

" Miss Jean," he said, with assumed concern, " I don't know how we are ever going to marry you off, unless in one of these wanderings of yours the god of the hill-top shall take visible form and woo you."

"Pray, Mr. Rand, have more consideration for your own energies than to undertake the task of marrying me off," she requested, icily. "Gods and men, I decline them both in advance."

He smiled, that indulgent smile men are wont to wear at the perversities of a handsome woman. Her attitude of affable contempt had a subtle allurement for the banker. He was weary of adulation and he was surfeited of simplicity. He admired youth in women,—there was no sense in a man's courting a death's head because he had a few gray hairs; he believed in freshness, bloom, fervor; but the gushing naïveté of the average girlhood was intolerable. That innocence which looked out upon the world and saw only a beautiful pageant, which contemplated men as Round Table knights in endless quests of honor,—his practical mind had no patience with such. But Jean, with that fine cynicism, whose growth he had watched with a secret delight, Jean had passed the mythological stage. Her early disappointment had given her a spice of distrust,—not the hard misanthropy he had known sorrow to leave in men,—but a tincture of disdain, as though she had surprised the world in a lie and henceforth scorned it.

"Ah, you must beware," the banker said, in a voice of fatherly counsel; "you are wrong to scout your lovers. You know how these things go in the old stories. The gentle maiden is the one who weds the prince, while the haughty demoiselle is left in solitude,—unless, indeed, she fares worse and is devoured by the beasts."

"Yes, I have often thought, considering the vibratory nature of the historic prince, that the haughty one must have blessed her fate," said Jean, archly.

"You are a doomed woman!" He shook his head with the conviction. "You are a doomed woman, for no man will ever find favor in your eyes."

Some sudden thought surprised the sentence on his lips, for he turned abruptly and looked at her. The sunlight was flashing down the ripples of her hair; and, as his critical gaze followed the curve of neck, and shoulder, and bust, his eyes narrowed, and he looked away meditatively over the cleared belt that lay between them and the town.

His mind had come upon an idea, and was limning thoughts which had floated heretofore only in detached shapelessness. It was time he was making himself a home and getting ready for the peaceful old age he had always projected. He was not strong; he remembered with new vividness the attack that had threatened his life only last year. He would need a nurse some day, he owned with regret; and what nurse would supply the needed devotion but a wife? He found himself, by some influence of contiguity, selecting the beautiful site just below them on the slope, and erecting in imagination a mansion worthy of his wealth and influence.

And who, of all he had met, could tread those imagined halls with the queenly grace of the woman beside him? He turned and surveyed her again with a closer scrutiny, and his eyes lingered upon her in satisfaction. What though she could not give him the full measure of love that another might,—her recurrent hours of depression convinced him that her heart was still with her lover,—still he could brook a rival as long as the rival was dead. He had no war to wage with his unfortunate assistant, Allan Brong. Besides, it would be a comfort, he was thinking, to possess a wife who was not committed to an impossible standard; ideals were dreadfully unpleasant things for a man to take into his household. He flattered himself that he might even surprise Jean's asperity with an occasional exhibition of a virtue she had not credited him with, which would make him feel quite of the redeemed.

And her beauty, remarkable as it was, had failed to supply her with the customary stock of vanity, in view of which women become so pettily exacting. Frederick Rand imagined he might tire of Aphrodite if she was constantly demanding admiration, or requiring him to attend upon her whims. He had a keen eye to personal comfort, and was seeing a fruitful promise in Jean's disdain of her own loveliness. She was not a woman to bewitch a man into folly,—into scaling cliffs or wading brooks, provoking him to execrate her bright eyes afterwards for the cold in his head,—and middle-aged men had a right to speculate upon possible colds in the head.

As he sat and catalogued his companion's virtues, he reached the conclusion that Miss Fennimore would prove a very satisfactory Mrs. Rand. Overleaping the preliminaries of courtship, proposal, and acceptance (which were trifles easy of arrangement), his mind assumed proprietorship, and began to consider the details of the mansion.

10

"Don't you think, Miss Jean, that slope yonder would be a sightly spot for a house?" he asked, pointing down the clearing.

She followed the direction of his finger, and studied the situation a moment.

"It would, indeed," she replied; "but if I were building I would set the house farther back, say on the ledge there, and terrace down from it. You remember how the view of the mountains is being cut off from our house, and a palace bereft of this landscape would be poorer than a cottage with it."

"Yes, I suppose in time, when the town is built up, the view will be prized because it can't be got. I don't lay much store by the outlook myself,—Hood and St. Helens are out of my line,—still, a man may as well take all he can get for the money. Suppose we walk down there now and note the lay of the land."

He extended his hand to assist her in rising, and with new interest drew her arm within his own.

"You see," Jean remarked, as they reached the ledge, "this eminence will command the country, however much the town may grow. And who would hedge himself between stone walls that could have, for the choosing, this glorious prospect? There is a broadening of the soul's sympathies in a view of open stretches; an elevating of desire in deepening skies and upreaching peaks. The sense of futility that haunts life vanishes in expanses, and the sublime becomes the real again."

The banker did not speak; heroics pertained evidently to the peaks, and both, as he said, were out of his line. Still, Jean's little rhapsody confirmed his purpose of building on the ledge. If the claims of the æsthetic were to be satisfied for a few rods of ground, by all means he would build his house upon the rock. He gazed down, his eye mapping in mechanical lines the limits of a goodly section, but Jean was looking out over the town asleep in the drowsy sunlight, and the river like a glistening snake winding its sinuous way among the grasses. Beyond, an occasional wheatfield threw its yellow spangle against the tawny robes of the forest, and off in the purple distance the mountains were fondling the sky. The sun-shaft had crept to the summit of the peaks, and spilled its fiery cup; streams of light were trickling down, burning their way across the snows, and burnishing the spears in the bristling fir hedges.

But the banker's thoughts were on more material issues, and he broke in ruthlessly upon her contemplation.

"What would you suggest as to the structure, Miss Jean?" he asked.

"Are you really thinking of building?"

"I am, indeed; and, since you have so graciously given me your opinion on the site, I am led to request your ideas on the house."

Jean was silent a space, and yet she was not collecting her disjointed theories on house-building; she was wondering what sudden whim had inspired him to this eccentricity.

"For the house, I am afraid I have few ideas to advance.

Broad piazzas and plenty of big windows would be all I should stipulate for. An architect would be better fitted than I to prepare designs for a bachelor's establishment."

"A bachelor's establishment!" he repeated, in disgust; "how can you suggest it?"

Then, realizing that he had not informed her of his intentions, he leaned over in an affectionate confidence quite different from his wonted gallantry and opened his lips to commit himself to her acceptance, when suddenly she started, rose, and without a word stepped lightly down the rocky ledge and stood beside Thurgar. For a moment her hand rested upon the gold of his hair, and she looked away with a pained desolation in her face. But the child by some secret sympathy rose also, and, putting his hand in hers, stood beside her. She clasped the little palm tightly, and slowly the beating of her heart grew calmed and she recovered herself.

Frederick Rand still sat upon the ledge, but she had no intention of renewing the situation. She drew out her watch, and, facing about, called merrily back to him,—

"You will be convicted of treason against your best friend to-day, surely; dinner was served half an hour ago."

He got up leisurely and came down the incline, and Jean could see under his complaisance a shade of perplexed irritation. But the suave amiability came back in a moment. Perhaps he realized that the time was inopportune for a declaration, since the dinner must be growing less eatable with every word. Proposing was only a matter of form: he felt as secure of the chosen Mrs. Rand as though they had been engaged from youth. Why, therefore, should he take any liberties with his digestion?

They walked home at a good, brisk pace, and the only evidence the banker gave that his mind still harbored its purpose was the remark he made as they entered the door,— and he made it calmly, as of a matter on which there was a perfect understanding,—

"I shall instruct my agent to purchase that site, Miss Jean; and I shall order designs which will be submitted later for your approval."

But she only bowed slightly and left him.

CHAPTER XVII.

"WE are to add a member to our family to-morrow," Mrs. Wright announced that evening to the household assembled at the dinner-table; "and I think we are going to find him a valuable acquisition."

"Some one must be gifted with wonderful powers of persuasion," said Mr. Todd, in suppressed pique. "I have sent five applicants myself after those rooms, but none succeeded in getting them. Who might the favored one be?"

"The new doctor. I don't know exactly how it came about," she volunteered, in explanation; "for I had decided some time ago to keep the rooms for Harriet. Perhaps Dr. Hild carries some opiate to opposition in that quiet manner of his; or, maybe," she added, laughing, "I am growing partial to fine-looking men."

"He is spoken of highly," observed the clergyman. "I have met him myself, and I found him, as you say, a trifle dignified for one not of the cloth, but pleasant. If he impresses every one as favorably as he has us, Mrs. Wright, he ought to make a good record here."

Frederick Rand was too much absorbed in other thoughts to interest himself in a conversation about a stranger; and Jean in her preoccupation caught the statement that a new inmate was coming to-morrow, but dismissed it again without mental comment. After dinner she returned to the privacy of her sitting-room, and gave herself up to reflections.

With the quick perception of womankind, she had divined the banker's intention, and the sudden impulse which had thwarted him was but an instinct of her nature's recoil. She could decide his suit without debating; she did not for an instant harbor any purpose but that of rejection; still his overture precipitated one of her depressed attacks. In the morning she kept her room, hoping the mood would pass by noon; but at noon it lingered still. She recalled, too, that to-day Dr. Hild was coming, and it was always a trial to meet strangers; so she kept to her seclusion.

"We will have to accuse Miss Jean of cultivating indisposition to-day, Dr. Hild, on purpose to test your skill," said the editor, in his gay, bantering way.

"Possibly, rather, it is another evidence of the economic principle that a need begets a supply, and a supply begets a need," said the doctor, genially.

After dinner, when in the pleasant evening weather every one went out,—the ladies to saunter about the grounds, the gentlemen to walk down for the late mail,—Jean crept softly down the stairs and entered the parlor.

She was desolate to-night, and she hungered for a word or a glance of affectionate interest. She crossed the room, and, standing before the picture of Martin Fennimore, looked up into the open, speaking eyes. Did he love her, her father? Did he know at what cost she had obeyed him? How she longed to pierce the silence,—the cruel, stony silence of the grave! She folded her hands together, and prayed that by some miracle of power the years might roll back and restore her one moment to his living presence, that she might hear again one word of tenderness and of love.

As she gazed upward, her eyes burning, her hands clasped, her head poised in entreaty, a man stepped out of the embrasured window and stood transfixed. He had seen beautiful women a-many in the world's famous capitals, but he had come to the confines to see a woman like this. For a long time he stood oblivious to everything but the exquisite vision before him; then suddenly he recalled that he was intruding upon a spirit's privacy; he stepped across the room to where she was, and paused. She did not hear his footstep, but slowly, by the magnetism of his personality, she became aware of his presence, turned, and their eyes met. He extended his hand, and in it she rested hers, without thought, naturally. It was one of those instinctive movements by which something in one soul expresses its kinship to another. In the deep current that underlies the conventional their spirits had met, and the great fact of affinity had uttered itself. He held her hand through that long moment unconfusedly; then, releasing it, he said, quietly,—

"You are Miss Fennimore? Let me introduce myself: I am Emory Hild."

"The new doctor?"

"The new doctor," he assented, with a faint smile. "You have been a little ill to-day, Mrs. Wright tells me. I hope you have recovered, and are well again."

There was an accent of shaded sympathy in his voice, but there was besides some strange influence that in the excited state of her mind acted upon her mesmerically. She was actuated by a sudden desire to throw herself upon his confidence; but, as she looked in his face, she closed her lips nervously to shut in the struggling words.

Unfrequently in women, more rarely yet in men, one finds an eye that looks out upon the world cheerfully, frankly, yet with a subtle penetration as though behind the visible it saw the essence. Such eyes by some reactive influence are endowed with a spiritual transparency; you look into them, and know henceforth how eyes are vehicles of thought and how a strong soul generates power.

As Jean looked into Emory Hild's face she felt herself charged with a sense of his mastery, and she glanced confusedly away.

"You are ill, Miss Fennimore, but—pardon me if I am presuming—the offices of a physician are, I fear, not exactly what you need. Will you not allow me the pleasure of serving you as a friend?"

He stood close beside her, and it seemed to Jean that her power of voluntary action was being drugged, and with a blind impulse of retreat, "No," she stammered; "I am only ill," and, turning away, she hurriedly left the room.

"A nervous organism," soliloquized Dr. Hild; "and a sympathetic mind,—two unwholesome possessions for a beautiful woman."

CHAPTER XVIII.

It was several weeks later that in the early evening the family was distributed as usual about the grounds. There was a slight change in the weather and the air was somewhat chilly. The clergyman was conversing with the young doctor, and his remark touched a subject which was creating just then considerable comment in the town.

"I understand the hospital has been placed under your direction, Dr. Hild," he was saying. "I want to congratulate you, and I want also to congratulate the hospital. Your profession is one that confers great opportunities for good."

"Yes," conceded the doctor; "though I suppose every medical man is alive to the provisional quality of the good he does. We remedy the existent evils, but their conditions are almost beyond our reach. I am daily more impressed with how deeply the physical is rooted in the moral, and the characters of men are, you know, beyond our province."

"I should think," said the minister, with a hesitation as of one who must suggest a remedy but has none quite adapted to the case,—"I should think your female nurses might be delegated to a little missionary service. The influence of woman is conceded to be elevating, and men in illness are impressible."

"Impressible! yes, but impressible through their judgment," Mr. Wright interrupted. He was wont to presume a little upon the good man's courtesy. "Men must be convinced through their reason, my friend, through their reason; and this special faculty is, alas! in abeyance in woman. She is incapable of logic, Mr. Gibbon; she quite disdains the syllogism, and she is a living contradiction of axioms. Science and philosophy know her only as an erratic meteor, so to speak,—a brilliant interloper that sets at defiance the order of the universe."

Dr. Hild was betrayed into a smile, but the clergyman simply bowed in response, and addressed himself again to the physician.

"Could you not inaugurate a little reform quietly, as I suggested?"

Dr. Hild was silent a moment in reflection.

"I have a fancy," he replied, "that with men of the lower orders, such as our hospital patients come from, the influence of woman is likely to be temporary. Purity and unselfishness are so generally associated with womanhood that the world has come to look upon them as feminine virtues. Now, feminine means to this class effeminate, and anything suggestive of weakness they not unnaturally despise. I think the most permanent good among such is to be done by a man who shall unite their own strong hardihood and virility to the virtue they deem incompatible with it,—a man who shall show a clean soul combined with perfect strength and manliness."

He was occupied with his remarks, and did not notice that

Mrs. Gibbon and Miss Fennimore had come up during the conversation and were standing close at hand listening.

"Do you think, Dr. Hild," the latter inquired, "that such a man is possible to this age?"

She regretted her question instantly, but it was spoken. He turned upon her a look in which surprise struggled with disappointment.

"Do you doubt it?" he asked.

"I do," she said, desperately, and turning she walked away.

She fancied, as her retreating gaze swept his face, that his expression was one of repulsion, and her heart passed under it into eclipse. Was he not such an one himself,—this calm, strong, clear-eyed man? That pained, wondering look sent into her doubt a sting of degradation, as no word had ever done. How he must despise her! What a narrow, distorted, warped thing her mind must seem to him! She longed to rush back and tell him that she did believe in goodness, for she believed in him; that she knew once more the ideal was not a fantasy, for she had found it in a living man, but she did not move.

Her remark had certainly given an unpleasant shock to Emory Hild's sensibilities. Distrust, suspicion, is chilling in man; in woman it is repellent. He had before noted the acrid humor of her mind, and it grated harshly upon him that such sentiments should come from such perfect lips. He was silent a moment now, and the minister, who divined the young man's thoughts, was studying how he should explain to him Jean's strange cynicism.

Thurgar Wright came upon them just then, and the physician, stretching out his hand, barred the boy's advance. The two had struck up a confidential acquaintance, and the little fellow, thus invited, drew near, and leaned familiarly against the doctor's shoulder.

"You have not heard of Miss Fennimore's early sorrow, have you, Dr. Hild?" said the minister, in a low voice, heedless of the child. He deemed it wrong that his companion's estimate should not consider this fateful factor.

"No, I have not," he answered, simply.

"It is very generally known, so I betray no confidence in repeating it. She was engaged some years ago, when she was scarcely seventeen, to a very promising young fellow, who was our friend's assistant in the bank." He pointed, as he spoke, to Frederick Rand, who had drawn a chair beside Jean, and was engaged in an animated conversation. "He was very devoted to her, as she was also to him," the minister continued; "but her father, old Martin Fennimore, who was a particularly obstinate man, was opposed to the match. He tried to prevail upon Miss Fennimore to give her lover up; but she had some of the old man's self-will herself, and refused. Before they were married Martin Fennimore died suddenly. His death produced a great impression on Miss Jean, and shortly after, in an impulse of loyalty, I suppose, she broke her engagement with Allan Brong. It has affected her whole life since, and he, poor fellow, never recovered from the blow. He took to drinking, and some months after he killed himself. Much is to be excused in Miss Fenni-

more," said the clergyman, meaningly, "in consideration of
the tragedy of Allan Brong."

"Everything is to be excused,—everything," said the
doctor, with warmth, "and I thank you sincerely for ac-
quainting me with it."

It was a story to stir a child's imagination, and Thurgar's
precocious mind had seized it eagerly. He slipped away
from Dr. Hild, and, running to his aunt, threw his arms
about her neck, in a mystified trepidation at this strange
catastrophe that someway enveloped her.

"Little Thurgar Wright was born about that time," continued the minister, his mind led back by the child's action,
"and Miss Jean took to the boy in her sorrow, and has been
like a mother to him since. Her nature, Dr. Hild, is as beautiful as her person, if one can read it aright, for her doubts
have not clogged the flow of her sympathies, and some day I
expect to see her restored to a confidence in the highest."

Emory Hild did not speak at once. When he did, the
words came slowly, almost sadly:

"The most solemn mystery of life to me is that one shall
sin and another shall suffer."

During the clergyman's recital Frederick Rand had stepped
back into the house. He returned now with a light wrap,
which he proceeded to adjust comfortably about Miss Fennimore's shoulders. It was surprising to himself how careful
he had grown of Jean since he had assumed proprietorship.
In the distraction of her thoughts she was scarcely conscious
of his presence, and allowed him to settle the wrap without

comment or hinderance. Dr. Hild's face took on an aspect of new wonder. Could it be that she was encouraging the attentions of that man? He was unwilling to linger near them, lest something should confirm the unpleasant suspicion; so he hastily bade the clergyman good-night and took his departure. As he passed the two, the banker was remarking, confidentally,—

"That site you chose for the house has been purchased, Miss Jean, and I included the land to the crest of the hill."

Emory Hild walked on up the steps, and his tread seemed heavier than was its wont. Another had caught the remark also, but Mrs. Wright was uncommonly affable that evening.

In the quiet of his room the doctor threw himself into a chair and looked out listlessly over the curved sweep of the river. He had remarked in the early morning that the glinting stream, coiling itself against the foot of St. Helens, was an inspiration, but to-night a chilly gloom had settled upon the waters and St. Helens was miles away. Why should the incidents of another's life overcast his? What was it to him that Jean Fennimore had loved, and probably still loved Allan Brong? What was it to him that she choose to receive the banker's addresses? He could not bring himself to believe that a woman whose every movement was an unconscious obeisance to the canons of both ethics and æsthetics could find anything akin in Frederick Rand; but why should the matter concern him at all? She had assumed with Emory Hild, since the night of their first meeting, that intangible aloofness which he interpreted as an avowal of her indifference, if not of her dislike; and he re-sented his own interest in a woman to whom that interest was unwelcome.

He snatched up a book and read aloud rapidly, but soon the sound of his voice had ceased, and he was sitting idly, watching the shadows creep out from the sombre corners. At last he jumped up and shook himself.

"Emory Hild, I'm ashamed of you," he ejaculated. "A man in your condition of health to be entertaining blue devils! A sound sleep and a long walk before breakfast—these shall be your prescription. I trust," he added, grimly, "the case may call for no severer treatment."

He retired according to direction, but the sound sleep did not come at his bidding, for throughout his dreams he was engaged in a feverish dance in which the wraith of Allan Brong was mixed up confusedly with the banker, Jean, and himself, and he woke too late for the walk which was to have completed his cure.

CHAPTER XIX.

" WILL you ride down, Mr. Wright?" the doctor asked of the philosopher, as they came out of the gate together, next morning. " I am going your way, and will drop you wherever you wish."

" Well, yes, I will avail myself, if you will pass the post-office."

He got into the carriage, and as they drove off he remarked, " I want to mail these letters myself in person. There are a few subjects, Dr. Hild, on which Mrs. Wright and I hold different opinions,—trifles, of course; no two could be more truly united than my wife and myself; but we are both somewhat tenacious of ideas. Now, Mrs. Wright holds to the judgment that I should give over my efforts for the sublime cause because they do not meet public favor, but, Dr. Hild, I am resolved to immolate myself at the stake of duty though the whole world oppose it."

" You are still hoping, are you," said the doctor, a trifle vacantly, " to have the Indians relieved of white influence?"

" That is the first condition of their usefulness, doctor,—a usefulness that every day of the present odious contact imperils. I sent some years ago to Washington a protest against the abuse, but the last administration through its double term was notoriously indifferent to the wants of the country. I have prepared here a memorial to Congress, asking an appropriation, and a petition to the Executive. I have also sent out a pamphlet to the various Indian agents asking their individual efforts to secure their withdrawal, and I have prepared for the leading papers a lengthy report setting forth our crying need for thinkers and the divine fitness of the savage. I expect now to see a general awaking of the public conscience against this treatment of our national ward. The American people are slow to rouse, doctor,—very slow to rouse; but, once awake, they move like an avalanche."

"Yes, it is hard sometimes, though, to convince others of what is self-evident to ourselves," the doctor remarked, evasively.

"I have tried to interest several of our capitalists here," Mr. Wright resumed; "but, between ourselves, Dr. Hild, the West is narrow,—the West is narrow. It has not grown to the large philanthropy of a liberal culture, or the broad sentiments that take in the ages. Mr. Rand, now,—he could make his name immortal by inaugurating this great work for science, but he prefers his miserable dimes. Still, I look to see our home capitalists follow liberally when the ball gets well in motion. This first appropriation that Congress contemplates will show that the statesmen of the country appreciate the situation, and the legislators will carry the moneyed men. I am expecting any day now to be called to Washington to assume the management of a new Bureau."

They reached the post-office at this juncture, and the apostle hesitated between his desire to attend personally to his mail, and the temptation to remain in the carriage and continue the conversation with his new victim. But the need of the nation was urgent: he stepped out, and, bidding the doctor good-morning, vanished within the building.

"What drivelling idiocy! And that man the husband of Mrs. Wright!" Emory Hild had food for reflection. "And what a pair, those two, to control the destinies of children!" he pondered, as he drove on. "Here is Harriet growing up without an idea beyond shining in society, while Thurgar is ignored entirely. Such parents make one despise the name. And they will reap in Thurgar the harvest they are sowing! That imaginative little mind is susceptible of much good, but susceptible also of an obstinacy in evil. Such natures owe their direction entirely to shaping influences,—but there is no time for character-moulding since calls must be returned and the savage saved to philosophy!"

By the time Dr. Hild had reached his office, his brows were contracted in a frown of disgusted contempt, but, as he tied the horses and ascended the steps, he broke into a low whistle which told that his healthy equilibrium was restored.

CHAPTER XX.

THE summer days rolled slowly into autumn, leaving to mark their passage nothing in the quality of an event, but influences and impressions that like the drowsy spirit of the sunshine lingered in emotion rather than in thought. To Jean these days were full of the sensuous peace one feels by the shore of a quiet lake where reflection stirs vaguely only to be lulled into dreamy languor by the soft lapsing of waters. Her habitual quiet was underlaid with a happiness that sent the old sparkle into her dark eyes and the old buoyancy into her manner. The world was coming to look less distorted as her faith in mankind revived. And she was sweetly accessible to faith since it had found such a winning embodiment in Emory Hild. It was her delight through these months to study him; to note how he watched his every utterance in that pride which rebelled against her influence, and yet how he was surprised into perpetual betrayals. She had meant to be very guarded herself, and yet, she fancied, two or three sudden, penetrative gleams portended a surmise that she was not altogether indifferent to him. There was a certain fascination in assuming that they suspected each other's feeling, even though her conscience disapproved the collusion.

But others of the household, she feared, had also grown suddenly acute in perception; for Frederick Rand had looked astonishment and displeasure when, the other evening, walking up to take a look at his new purchase, he beheld them on the ledge above, enjoying the sunset together. As she sat idling over her piece of sewing now, she remembered that the banker had invited her to go boating to-night, and she was pythoness enough to know that he meant to bring his suit to a crisis. Well, she must give up her evening to him, but her afternoon she could devote as she choose, and her mind went back to Emory Hild till her cheeks grew red and her lips sweetly tremulous.

There was a light knock at her sitting-room door, a quiet opening, and her sister entered, before Jean could dismiss the tell-tale color or conceal the smile. Two gray eyes surveyed her sharply, but Margaret made no comment on the evidence. She only drew her chair over close, remarking, as she did so,—

"That needle-work makes very slow progress."

Jean did not answer; the needle-work was not the object of Margaret's call, and that imperious lady was not thus given to studying the approaches. Her companion began to be unaccountably ominous, but she was not left long to her suspense.

"I have been meditating a little interview with you for several days," Margaret said, turning from the stitching, "and to-day the visit has been precipitated by an interested party."

Jean glanced up, but in sudden obstinacy lowered her eyes again.

i

"My fair sister is unaware, I suppose," Margaret observed, blandly, "that she has made a conquest of our worthy banker."

"Your fair sister is very indifferent to the conquest of the worthy banker," Jean replied, frigidly.

"I suspected so." The smile upon Mrs. Wright's lips was unconstrained, but there lurked in it a deepening cunning. "She is probably not quite so indifferent to the conquest of our clever young doctor." Her eyebrows were raised a trifle, and she looked sharply into the face that bent above the sewing.

"No, I am not indifferent to Dr. Hild," Jean said, in wilful defiance. "I love him, and I shall love him as long as I live."

"I commend your taste; he is a handsome man. And you will marry him?"

Her head drooped; she was silent. The question was a cruel one; she had avoided it even in her musings.

"No, I will not marry him," she said at last, very slowly. "I love him; I will not marry him."

"You are right, Jean, because——"

The young girl waved her hand angrily; she would not allow Margaret's cold analysis of what touched her so intimately, and the discreet sister obeyed the gesture and was silent.

"And what do you intend to do with Mr. Rand?" she asked, at last.

"What shall I do with him? Leave him to his horses and his money-bags. They want him; I don't."

" Jean !"

" Hold, Margaret," she called, impetuously, " do not interfere here. Keep your soul clean of any deeper wrong. I
obeyed you once; do not require at my hands another sacrifice."

" It is not I,"—the voice was gentle, propitiating,—" it is
not I that require it; it is destiny. You know my condition;
Caleb Wright will never be anything but a pauper; and the
children,—who shall make their futures? Harriet is a girl,
pretty and clever,—I can manage for her; but Thurgar,—who
shall provide for him? Nature is in arrears to me in the
matter of my maternal sentiments," she said, with slow
meaning, " and I am just callous enough to be anxious to
throw him upon your devotion. He is so fond of you;
he relies upon you so; he seems to expect so much from
you !"

Every word was sped with a skill that measured accurately
its carrying force, and the young girl looked up fearfully.

" What do you wish of me, Margaret ?"

" Place Thurgar where he can defy the world," she said,
with low incision. " Give to him what I cannot,—education,
position, wealth, power: he shall need them all some day.
The means is offered you now; it may never be offered you
again. You must marry Frederick Rand."

" Marry Fre-der-ick Rand !" The syllables fell one by
one, as though she had dropped them from her upraised
fingers. There was a chilled deadness in the tones as though
the thought froze the very current of her speech.

"It is a hard, ugly request, dear," Margaret allowed, "but —but—you love my boy, do you not? He it is who requires it? You love my Thurgar?"

Jean was sitting very still. The whiteness was creeping from her forehead into her cheeks and lips and leaving her face ashen. From her seat beside the window, she could look down to where the boy, weary of play, had thrown himself upon the grass. His fair curls lay like a nimbus about his head, and his eyes—those strange, dark eyes— were searching the cloud-flecked heavens. As she glanced out he turned and looked up at her fixedly. Was it her fancy that read in his look an appeal, or did he by the mysterious sympathy of love feel and reflect her trouble? Surely the eyes were very earnest for boy's eyes; and, gazing into them, all balancing of doubts, all thought of herself, of her new love and her new sorrow, were overborne, and Thurgar was supreme.

Margaret watched the silent drama a moment. "The child has become his own advocate," she murmured, and slipped away, leaving her sister alone to the inevitable issue.

The walls of her room seemed to the hapless wrestler to be slowly contracting; she panted under a crushing pressure; she gasped at air that was thick and stifling, for a numbness was creeping over her senses. She reached her hand to draw herself to the window, but with a sudden change of purpose she snatched up her hat and darted through the door. The rapid motion revived her, and she hurried along the hall and down the stairs. She could hear at the front door some of the gentlemen returning to dinner, so she glided hastily out at the side-entrance and took her way alone into the forest.

The sun was perched upon the western hills, and sent its glory in a line of vivid yellow along the path. The narrow grass-grown trail was transformed into a mellow sunbeam, through which she walked with unblinking eyes. It wrapped her about with its crocus robe until she grew warm, but the warmth was in the blood alone. She could see through the dense growth of trees, here and there, a shaft of gold, and a feathery film of light sifting down like a fine rain upon the mosses. She could hear the birds flinging out their transports in ravishing song, and she could catch the light flitting of feet across the untrodden woodways. The world was bright, full of active, happy life, and not a leaf fluttered into shadow for her coming. Her trouble was an alien thing; her human heart was unanswered of the forest. She reached the crest of the hill and looked away. Everything was still; the mountains were beguiled of their distance and their duskiness. Then her eye wandered down and caught the dancing gleam of the river. It was slipping off from the busy town with its fretting wharves, and hurrying to the unfettered way beyond. She followed its course around the bend, watching it enviously, for it had left its past, and was journeying to its future in oblivion. It drew her by its onward motion, and slowly she descended the slope, crossed the woods, and took the path leading north. She shivered visibly as she came out upon the bank and held her eyes resolutely to the water, but the fascination was strong, she

12

turned and cast one furtive glance in among the trees. Yes, there was the rendezvous; she almost fancied she could hear Allan Brong's footsteps hurrying to meet her. She drew her eyes away again, and fled in haste along the stream.

Never since that night of long ago had she visited this spot, but everything was familiar. It brought back in renewed vividness what time had been laboring to efface. How she hated the man who was associated to her with every foot of these woods! Nothing but pain was linked with his memory,—pain and bitterness and foreboding. But her mind, in its oscillation, leaped from Allan Brong to that other whose presence had power to fill every pulse with delight. Her thought reached out to him now, and spent itself in a wild waste of longing.

As she advanced the forest became less dense, for some enterprising settler was making a clearing. A little within, the road was visible, keeping the trend of the bank, but Jean's gaze avoided it, and followed the line of the river.

A low cloud of dust came sweeping from the direction of the town, and was the only herald of a span of grays whose hoofs sank echoless into the heavy sand. As they sped past the stretch of thinned timber, they were reined in so suddenly that the dust swirled up and enveloped everything in obscurity. When it cleared away, the carriage had turned and was moving off homeward, and a tall figure was stepping out of the road and taking his way towards the river.

In her feverish rush of emotion, Jean was startled by the sound of footsteps. She glanced up, and—in the moment of surprise she had advanced with both hands extended to Emory Hild. Instantly, in abashed confusion she sought to withdraw them; but he intercepted her, and, taking in his firm clasp both the little, reluctant palms, said, with a kindling warmth,—

"I am glad you are not going to say I have intruded. I feared you might have wandered off here to be alone, and would resent my coming; but I saw you from the road yonder, and the temptation was not to be resisted."

He smiled, and there was a sort of defiance in his smile which would forestall any censure he might have deserved.

"I did come to be alone," she allowed, frankly, "but—I was thinking of you, so your presence cannot well be an intrusion."

"Thinking of me!" he said, with quick intentness. "I would scarcely have dared to hope for that. Come," as they turned and walked slowly back, "can't I prevail upon you to tell me in what capacity I was admitted to your thoughts?"

He was leading into dangerous paths, and her conscience sounded its sharp note of warning.

"No, no," she said, with faltering energy, "I dare not."

She was fearful of herself to-night, and she knew that safety was not waiting for her by the side of Emory Hild.

"I must go back," she persisted. "I have an engagement. We must not stay here together."

But in the antagonism of purpose and desire she did not hasten her pace, though her manner was alert and anxious.

"An engagement." He suspected with whom, and the smile was changed in his face to a frown. She would escape from him and hurry to an appointment with Frederick Rand. And yet he knew she cared nothing for the banker. Why was she thus fickle? Did she care for him? was he deceiving himself? or did she still cling to her old lover, Allan Brong? This uncertainty was distracting.

"Why must we not stay here together?" he asked, obstinately. "Indeed, if you will forgive my insistence, we must stay here, for there is something I must know, and you only can tell me."

They had left the open bank and were advancing along the path through the bit of intervening woods. He led her across to a fallen tree and seated himself.

"Come," he said, with gentle resoluteness, "and sit here by my side, and answer what I shall ask you."

He took her hand and drew her towards him, but she only stood in tremulous indecision. Her heart was beating violently, and her quick breathing told of a conflict of emotions. She must give him up to-night; she must carry henceforth only widowed memories in her breast. Might she not yield once to the sway of his presence? Conscience struck its authoritative "No!" but the close leading of his hand was stronger. With a low cry she sank beside him and was folded in his arms.

"Jean, my Jean," he whispered, triumphantly, "you do love me?"

"I love you, I love you," she faltered.

He bent his head, and their lips met in a rapturous consecration.

"And I love you, now, and forever, my Jean, my queen, my love, my wife."

She raised her eyes, quivering with their weight of happiness, and—she started, she glanced about. They were sitting in that fatal spot,—in the very seat where she had sat with Allan Brong. With a cry of horror, she sprang up and stepped away.

"Your wife,—yours? Never! never! never!"

Emory Hild rose in dismay. What strange power possessed her to make her a creature of such contradictions?

"But, Jean," he said, beseechingly, "you will explain,—you will tell me why, when you love me, you will not marry me?"

But she shrank back, and a wild, hunted look was her only answer.

"Jean, Jean!" he pleaded, "tell me, trust me. My love is strong enough to bear all things now, for I know that you love me."

But she only stared at him with the same startled, stricken gaze.

"Come; he is waiting. Come, come!" she said, excitedly, as she moved forward.

A light flashed across his mind. He was too late; the other had offered first, and she had accepted him.

"Jean!" he cried, grasping her arm, "tell me, tell me,—you are going to marry him?"

"Yes."

The word came out hard and hopeless, and the young man sank back upon the seat and leaned his head upon his hand. Presently he rose and stood beside her. He was painfully, oppressively calm. "Each soul must follow its own call," he said. "One cannot judge for another. I trust you because I love you. Good-by."

Only for one moment he held her against his heart; then they turned, and in silence they walked home. As they neared the house, they could see the banker leaning against the gate, now and again casting his eyes impatiently along the road. As they appeared, a shade of uneasiness crossed his face; he lifted his hat to the doctor, but addressed himself to Jean.

"Did you forget me?" he asked, with smiling reproach.

"No," she answered, quietly. "I am sorry if I kept you waiting. I will be ready in a few minutes."

She passed on into the house and returned with her gloves and a light shawl. Frederick Rand relieved her of the shawl; and, bowing good-by to her late companion without raising her eyes, she departed. A couple of hours later, the two strolled leisurely back; and, as they came up the walk, Emory Hild could catch from the window the echo of his rival's laugh, and it was very merry. At breakfast he noted upon Jean's hand the gleam of a superb diamond, and he knew that the rich man was the victor.

CHAPTER XXI.

IMMEDIATELY upon the shelving summit of the rocky spur appeared those mysterious traceries which are the prophecy of a house. Curiosity, in the guise of the banker's townsmen, assumed forthwith the office of inspector, and scrutinized every foot of construction with a zeal that might have implied a personal concern. But the zeal was a manifestation only of their interest in Portland's wealthiest citizen, and of their jealousy for the town's honor, which required that their individual expectations be satisfied. Even the most exacting, however, seemed willing to allow that Frederick Rand was acquitting himself of his duty sumptuously.

And when, two months later, in the old Fennimore home was celebrated a wedding which eclipsed in elegance all that had been known in the civic history, the family was invested with dignities which it could not have arrogated in Martin Fennimore's most imperial days.

"Ah, the old man had a long sight," was the sentiment of his neighbors, drawn by recent events to discussing anew those of by-gone times. "The old man had a long sight. Miss Jean was bait for bigger fish than Allan Brong; and why should she take the man when she might have the master? Martin Fennimore was a deep one,—a deep one." But along their comment ran a current of compassion which vented itself here and there in an articulate "Poor Brong!"

The bells were still pealing as the bridal party drove through the town. They were off for the tour,—a long one, which should give time for the completion of the house; and hats went up and hurrahs rang out all along the way, for cheers were the people's "God-speed!" to the two thus merrily gliding out to their new life together.

It was with a strange blending of emotions that Emory Hild watched the departure of the woman who had loved him, yet had become the bride of another. Sometimes he regretted that his sense of honor had prevented him from reasoning with her; but his judgment silenced the regret. Her own ideal of right must guide, and her own standard of duty. Again he was fired with a purpose of money-getting, for what could have induced her marriage unless that old command of her father's? What had doomed him to this desolation but his want of riches? But he put that thought away like the other. Money was not the end of his life; he would not stoop to make it so at Martin Fennimore's command.

Such suggestions were but the poor allurement of a spirit inapt at tempting; but a wilier craftsman was at hand, a master in seduction, who queried tauntingly, why did he remain here? Was it for the penitential pains of beholding his love's return, and her daily life as the wife of Frederick Rand? Only a zealot courted torture. His inheritance which he had invested on the growing business street would furnish an income ample for his wants; why not retreat now, and spare himself the future? But he recalled the beds of pain where the eyes of the sick and the dying turned to him in unspoken faith,—would he forsake them? And Thurgar,—Thurgar, who in his loneliness had flown upstairs to the only friend left, and cried himself to sleep upon Dr. Hild's shoulder,—he was lying there now; the man looked down into the boyish face,—could he desert him? Caleb Wright was indifferent to the lad; was his destined successor likely to be less so? Could the banker inspire an ardor for anything that was earnest and heroic, when his ideal of life touched nothing higher than his own gratification? Emory Hild settled his head back firmly on his shoulders; Jean loved the boy; Thurgar needed him; he would stay.

CHAPTER XXII.

THE house on the ridge had reached completion. The curiosity of the populace had fed upon its progress, and pronounced the structure goodly both in plan and execution. But curiosity, like gossip, is wont to grow whatsoever it may feed upon, and now the public appetite was waiting harpy-like to seize upon the details of the furnishings. Bales and boxes were arriving by every steamer, but they were transferred immediately to the house to be opened within its privacy; so no chance had been afforded of even a stolen peep at the trappings. Now, however, the day for Frederick Rand's return had come, and the party whom Mrs. Wright had invited to meet the banker and his bride and escort them home sat in their carriages, impatiently watching the cables tossed across to the wharf and the wheel frothing the water as the huge steamer settled to its moorings.

The decks were lined with faces; hands and handkerchiefs were waving, and here and there some eager one leaned down over the rail and chattered excitedly to friends on the landing below. The gang-plank was thrust out, the crowds surged ashore, cabs and omnibuses were loaded and driven away, and still the carriages and their occupants waited. Then Mrs. Wright, who had gone aboard to welcome the arrivals, returned with the chilling information that they had failed to appear.

142

The enthusiasm of the guests ebbed visibly, but their disappointment was politely veneered, and when, in lack of an alternative, Mrs. Wright transferred the festivities to her own house, the party drove thither in the pretence that the arrangement was equally pleasing.

"Our friends have deserted us," commented Mrs. Todd, with a shake of the head. "It is clear that soft-voiced sister of yours, Mrs. Wright, has become enamored of the land of gold and orange-groves."

But her husband's explanation was more practical. "A man can't be expected," he said, "to reckon on his movements closer than a week or two, in these days of slow stages and uncertain sailing. They probably failed to connect with the steamer."

A couple of weeks later, however, the overland mail brought a letter which sent Mrs. Wright posting at her horses' best speed into the town. She ascended to Dr. Hild's office, knocked smartly on the inner door, and entered.

"Mr. Rand begs you to hold yourself ready to attend him," she said, speaking very rapidly. "He is suddenly taken ill, —Mrs. Rand doesn't say just what is the matter,—but they have been making home by easy stages, and are due, as I figure it, to-night. I am on my way over to the house to prepare for them, and I stopped in a moment to tell you."

She hurried out again, and Dr. Hild could hear her carriage-wheels rasp the curb in their impetuous speed round the corner.

The rich man returned that night, but it was not the

splendid coming he had pictured. No ringing huzzahs greeted him by the way; no smiling friends crowded to whisper their adulation or swell his triumph. He wondered himself if he could be the same man who, suave and affable in his vigor, had passed along these streets such a few short months before. Men envied him that day; did they envy him now?

As he lay among the cushions in his luxurious chamber, and followed with his eyes the quiet figure that stepped so softly, adjusting a pillow now, now raising or lowering the coverlet,—despite his stinging sense of failure, he congratulated himself as a man who had circumvented fate. He had been provident in season; he had taken unto himself a wife, and none too soon to meet this insidious attack.

Furthermore, his wife was vindicating his judgment of her fully, for she was showing herself the most untiring of nurses. Indeed, Frederick Rand fancied sometimes that this strange woman was growing to care for him now in his dependence, so solicitous she seemed for his recovery. He wished for her sake that the physicians might hold out more hope, but the best they could offer was that, while at any time the end might come, on the other hand he might linger for years in his present condition. Not a bright prospect, he confessed, but so much more tolerable than it would have been without the sympathetic presence of Mrs. Rand that he grew quite resigned to his perfunctory existence.

It never occurred to him to pity the young wife whom he had condemned to the irksomeness of a sick-room. His demands were not restrained or his exactions tempered by any sparing tenderness. In health he might have proved the indulgent, amiable husband he had always pictured himself; but in illness, in this treacherous condition when, he reasoned, his very life might at any moment pay the forfeit of remitted care, could he be expected to consider another? He esteemed his wife; he had anticipated for her many years of pleasure before she should be called to the duty of attendant; but, since destiny had set her lot thus,—why, she must accept it. It was all a matter of business to the banker now. Jean was proving a dutiful wife, and he expected to prove a dutiful husband. No one should say he had failed to do honorably by Mrs. Rand; she would be paid in full, liberally,—why, therefore, should he spare her?

And she, his bondwoman, had no thought of murmuring. She was too conscious of the debt on her own side to think for an instant that any tax of her husband's could restore the balance. If he did not love her, at least he loved no other, and she was glad if, in some small measure, she could requite her lack of affection by fulness of service. Ah, self-surrender has its pain, Jean, and its numbness, but it leaves no regrets. Broaden your charity, temper your indulgence, and strain your patience, for the desolate days of the winter are over, and before the rains have returned Frederick Rand has crossed his threshold a second time; four strong men have borne him out again, and he has need of your service no longer.

CHAPTER XXIII.

THERE was food for gossip now to all the town. Even conservative, unmeddlesome people, like demure Mrs. Gibbon, were drawn into an incidental discussion of the death of the banker and the future of his young wife.

"Poor thing!" observed the clergyman's wife, to her friend Mrs. Todd, as they sat together in the sitting-room of Jean's old home, "she has had but a sorry married life, for all its auspicious opening. To be bereft of her husband so soon, what a calamity!"

"Yes, but calamities are made more bearable by the inheritance of such a fortune," said her friend, shrewdly. "You remember we used to think Miss Fennimore unworldly enough to choose Dr. Hild in preference to the banker; but she turned out more politic than her friends suspected. It is not impossible that when she chooses again, Dr. Hild may be more fortunate."

"Yes, perhaps, in time," said the other, hesitatingly. She felt guilty of a little breach of principle in canvassing another alliance for Mrs. Rand thus soon after her husband's death; but she compromised with her conscience by assuming a low tone of confidence.

"Dr. Hild must have cherished some hope," she observed, "he has been so blind to other attractions."

146

" Blind !" ejaculated Mrs. Todd, with a sparkle of contempt for her friend's simplicity; "that man's depth evokes my profoundest admiration. He will see nothing but what he wants to see. I believe he has bewitched the town,—at least, the susceptible, female half of it,—and he goes about looking so reserved and unconscious! Ah, he's clever. He'll bewitch Mrs. Rand like the rest, and we'll see another wedding—mark my prophecy—before the year's out."

Jean Fennimore had been a true wife to her husband; no whisper had ever come to link her name with any but Frederick Rand's. And yet, now that he was gone, the judgment of the astute Mrs. Todd seemed to be the judgment of the town. The romance of Jean's unmarried days was recalled, and nothing seemed more fitting than that love in the person of the popular young doctor should triumph at last in the possession of wealth and beauty.

The general eye took to surreptitiously noting the occasions of the doctor's visits to the house on the hill, and the general voice to speculating upon them. But the judgment of the gossips was one of censure. Dr. Hild was lax, it decided,—criminally lax,—for his visits were both unfrequent and short. Though the months passed to the fullest that any grief could demand for its season of mourning, they could not perceive that the two were approaching an understanding, or that any change had come in their manner to each other.

There is a contagion in public opinion. Perhaps, though unspoken, it was this that turned Emory Hild's mind into the same channel. He had never tried to solace himself with the delusion that another could fill Jean's place in his affections. Though the banker had lived to old age to claim his wife, yet must she remain to Emory Hild the love loved forever, though lost. Now, however, hope was beginning to steal softly a-tiptoe back into his heart. "Why should she not be mine?" he was inwardly querying. "She is rich, she cannot feel condemned to marry wealth again, and I have myself, in investments and practice, an ample competence."

Still he hesitated. "I love you, I love you." Memory echoed the faltering words she had spoken on the eve of her engagement, but did she love him still? He would wait patiently till some token, some word or glance should encourage him to renew his suit. But though he waited, and though he hoped, the encouragement never came. She was kind, she was courteous, but she never moved the line of intercourse a hair's breadth in advance of the conventional.

At times Emory Hild's courage failed him. An evil sprite would steal to his ear to whisper as of old, "She has forgotten; you are nothing to her now. Her heart overleaps the years, and clings only to her first love, Allan Brong." But someway his soul was not to be convinced.

These visits to her were growing harder and more constrained. To have upon his lips an avowal, a petition, and yet be held back by that old indefinable aloofness,—as inflammables gather sometimes from unknown sources the sudden heat which strikes them into flame, so latent emotions are mysteriously kindled and break forth into speech. There was no visible reason why after taking his leave, and reaching the drawing-room door, in one of his brief, formal calls, Dr. Hild should suddenly pause and turn about again; but the slumbering purpose had awakened in full impellent force, and with quick decision he stepped back and stood beside her.

"Jean," he asked, precipitately, "am I never to speak?"

She looked up. There was no surprise in her face, only a dull pity, and she did not reply.

"Are you not satisfied of my faithfulness? Must I wait to be further tested?"

She sighed, gently, a little wearily.

"You do not love me? Do not tell me that. Oh, do not tell me that you have forgotten."

For answer, she took his hand and folded it warmly in both of hers.

"I do love you,—more than my life,—but—but—trust me, Emory,—do not urge me to what is wrong."

He stood still, and looked away in helpless despair. This mystery that had shut him out before, and that faced him now again,—what was it? Not Martin Fennimore's will: Jean was rich, and he was no longer poor. Not her love for Allan Brong,—that was gone. She loved him; she confessed it, and yet,—and yet, he was again rejected.

"Tell me what lies between us," he cried, passionately. "Nothing can shake my love for you, and nothing shall separate us."

The expression of her face changed to that hunted distress he had caught there before.

"Tell me,—tell me; I must know," he cried, desperately.

But she turned away as in fear. "No, I cannot." She covered her face with her hands, muttering confusedly, "For one lives and one is dead."

"What do you mean?" he asked, excitedly. "One lives and one is dead,—what do you mean?"

"Nothing, nothing. What am I saying!"

Her eyes dilated painfully; her suffering spoke in every feature. Emory Hild sank back into his chair, with an overwhelming sense of defeat. This mystery, whatever it was,—how could he pierce it? Whom did it concern? Had her late husband bound her in any way? He was capable of it, Emory Hild conceded. Was it connected with Allan Brong, or was it still some fancied duty to her father? It was all dark, dark, and to look for light was hopeless. He sat absorbed in perplexity, and he might have sat so all night, but Jean had recovered herself; she stood before him again in her customary, quiet self-control.

"Forget what may have escaped my lips in a moment of excitement," she said, dully, "and for my sake leave the past to its own silence. Do not seek to influence me against my conscience. I love you with my whole soul, but we can never be to each other more than we are now. If you can forget me and marry another, I shall rejoice in your happiness. If not,—I have only my love to give you; in time and in eternity it is yours." She bent, and pressed her lips a moment against his brow, then silently she turned and left the room.

The hand that ministered at the bedside of the sick and the dying had lost none of its gentleness or its skill. The voice was soothing and cheery as was its wont, but the lines about the strong mouth began to deepen, the eyes had caught the weight of a lingering shadow, and people remarked how early Dr. Hild was growing old.

CHAPTER XXIV.

THURGAR WRIGHT had passed through the various phases incident to the section of life's orbit known as youth, and was gliding now into the quadrant of nodes,—young manhood. Twenty years had passed since with the protest of a mouth ready drawn for wailing, he had been handed about in the old Fennimore house and received—with baby ungraciousness, it must be confessed—the compliments of the guests.

He was a creditable product, this hardy, generous, ardent young fellow; not given to envying the saintly joys of the ascetic or to paying for spiritual exaltation in usury of knee-service, but nevertheless a healthy, vigorous soul. The constant dripping of Emory Hild's influence had filtered largely from the young man's nature that sediment of evil which settles down in character as dregs from even the purest wine. But with all his easy affinity for the enjoyable, there was in Thurgar Wright a sterling fibre of independence. It had often, through the years, given a sudden wrench to his pleasures to know that they were supported by one whose gentle love simulated a claim their relationship did not warrant. Now, as the potentials of life opened before him, his independence began to be very assertive. So when, during that interval of mental moodiness which accompanies the choosing of a career, Dr. Hild inquired if he had yet succeeded in formulating his desires, he could answer positively,—

152

"If I have not decided what I shall be, I have at least decided what I shall not be."

"Which narrows the range of choice by one, at least," said the doctor, good-humoredly. "Come, let us know which has aroused such an aggressive opposition. Not my honorable profession, I trust?"

"No, not the medicine. Indeed, I didn't mean,"—he seemed struggling for an expression that might soften any appearance of obstinacy in his remark,—"I didn't mean to oppose any of the suggestions. If Aunt Jean needs my service, it would be poor gratitude to refuse it."

"Ah, then it is the banking you dislike," Jean remarked, in quick inference. He had expected her to show disappointment, but that long-drawn breath seemed more one of relief.

"You are specially fitted for the banking, though, Thurgar boy," she said. "The details you will master readily, and ultimately I will make over the business to you. I have enough besides, and I have kept the bank solely for this purpose, dear?"

"You are my good angel always." He lowered his eyes to hide how her generosity had touched him. "My devoted angel. You have been to me, you and Dr. Hild, more than parents; yet I cannot conquer the wish that my future be of my own making. Only so shall I be happy; I can be a dependant no longer."

A gleam of delight glowed in the eyes of Emory Hild, but Jean looked up anxiously in that quick shock which

marks the first realization that a child is a distinct entity.
That Thurgar could meditate a future apart from natural
provisions, and independent of visible circumstances and
opportunities, was a complexion of idea she could not in-
terpret. She felt that the goodly structure which she had
reared had suddenly discovered its treacherous base and was
toppling about her. Thurgar's clean·young hands shrunk
from a touch of the banker's fortune, but Emory Hild was
unbiassed by any inconvenient knowledge. He could remember far enough back to appreciate and respect the lad's
fervid courage. Youth is the season of aspirations, of high
endeavor. It craves achievement, conflict, the full activity
of powers, the enlistment of the complete being. So he
said seriously, but with the tone of light banter he always
used with him,—

"A future of your own making! You are leading us to
expect something very unique, Thurgar. May we ask in
what mould you think of casting it, or is that, too, to be
something original?"

Thurgar looked up, a little nettled at this humerous reception of what was so solemn to him, but his mobile face soon
lighted again in the genial warmth of the doctor's glance.

"I haven't decided at all what I shall be," he said. "If I
should follow my own preference, I would have to disregard
all your propositions, for I would choose,—I know you will
be disgusted now,—I would choose,—yes, I would,—the
cattle business. But that requires capital, and I wouldn't
ask it from my father,—even if he were likely to give it."

"Thurgar, Thurgar!" Jean called, reproachfully. "Have I loved you all these years only for this? How you grieve me!"

"No, no, Aunt Jean." He tossed his hand impatiently. "I won't have your money," he said, sturdily.

"My money! It is your own. Why did I mar——?" She paused. She had forgotten herself. When she glanced up, Emory Hild's eyes were fastened upon her with a look that conjured up the old forest and the shadowy path by the river, and Thurgar had put his arm about her in a reverent sympathy that told his quick young mind had supplied what she suppressed. Dr. Hild hastened to relieve the situation by addressing the young man.

"I think, Thurgar," he said, quietly, "you owe something to your aunt's feelings in this matter. You must see how deeply you wound her in refusing her money. I can understand and I heartily approve your purpose of independence, but your start in life you can at least accept as a loan without compromising your dignity."

"A loan, a loan! Well, now, a loan did not occur to me. That would be at least a shade more honest than taking it outright. I seem destined to be always your pensioner," he said, with boyish wistfulness; "but, if you are willing to consider the money a loan, I shall be tempted, I confess, to take it, for I should like the business, of all things."

"Then we shall hold the considering done," said Dr. Hild, with his decisive, professional manner; "and look upon you henceforth as an embryo cattle king. I believe, though I am not an authority upon the subject, that the next thing after the money is the range, and I suggest that you start out early next month and take a trip up through the eastern country to search out a favorable location. You could study the methods and management, and you might run across a band it would be well to buy outright."

Thurgar's face was alight with pleasure. Dr. Hild had such an effective way of making up one's mind for one's self! His bold plunge into details made it seem to Thurgar as though the preliminary hesitation had never existed, but that he had contemplated this move from infancy. Then, what larger concession to his independence could be imagined than this of the whole North-west from which to choose his range with absolute freedom in investment and control?

He was consumed with impatience to be off. The days seemed to him conspiring for his delay, so idly did they dawdle along, but to his aunt they seemed hurrying forward with malicious rapidity. So, to the one tardily, to the other with obtrusive speed, the day arrived at last; and Thurgar, standing in his traveller's garb over against the background of the autumn dawn, kissed his aunt, pressed Dr. Hild's hand hard, and went blithely out into the world.

CHAPTER XXV.

The little steamer that cast her moorings and slipped out into the stream seemed to Thurgar that morning some wide-winged bird that might suddenly spread her snowy pinions and bear him aloft to realms of aërial enchantment. No searing experience had come to him yet to fling its fiery tongue across the gossamer web of illusions that, spider-like, youth weaves about itself. The world moved visibly to beneficent ends; men were high-souled and generous. To be sure, he had seen, with Dr. Hild, distortions of human kind that might have shaken a less hearty faith, but he thought of them always as moral cripples, men whom in a moment of mental torpor some accident had overtaken and left monstrosities, unfit for responsible service. For himself, he had known no such torpor. The faculties of reason and conscience were always dominant. Sin existed, and worked its baleful way, but it was a thing insulated from himself, with which he could have no organic connection. He had never felt the force of a powerful temptation, but was full of the confident trust that comes of personal innocence. Men were knightly, life was a thing of sublimities, and the world, —ah, the world was a new-born splendor!

The sun had sent out his beams to clear the path for his coming, and now in radiant glory he swept to his throne upon the mountain and tossed the light of his regal smile across the valley. The trailing robes fell from his footstool and lay along the peak,—flaming snows on the mountains, and flaming snows in the sky, for the clouds were alight, and the world was glowing in the first flush of morning.

Down on the quiet river the steamer was cutting its iridescent wedge. The water climbing up the bow was falling over in a scintillating shower, and astern the foaming waves were tossing up a spray of diamonds.

Along the banks the cotton-woods nodded and swayed, coquetting in arch modesty with both lovers,—the light and the shade. They bent now for another conquest, and kissed to Thurgar their perfumed hands and waved their dimpled farewell in a flutter of gleaming leaves. A smile was on his lips. As the steamer sped out of the Willamette he turned and bowed his head as though sending back thanks to conscious hearts that had thrilled to his own light happiness.

At the portage of the Cascades, the little steamer was abandoned for a six-mile jaunt by rail; then the upper river boat took them on again to the narrow gorge of the Dalles. Navigation ended here; so, procuring a horse and equipping himself thoroughly for his journey, Thurgar struck down into the Deschutes valley, taking the road to Prineville. From Prineville he crossed leisurely to the John Day, and over Lone valley through Hepner to the Umatilla. It was a noted cattle district; the rolling hills were heavy with rich, yellow, bunch grass, and the coulées in among the spurs of the Blue were visions for the eye of an artist. More than once Thurgar was tempted to abandon a further search and enter upon the possession of one of these picturesque spots, but the roving spirit was on him now; he turned again, and rode down into the valley of the Grande Ronde, and the Wallowa.

Every mile of the way deepened his wonder. Surely, beyond this there was nothing. He might traverse the continent, and find no rival to the Grande Ronde. He was enamoured, and wandered about for weeks in an exuberance of sensuous delight. Two or three bands he found in which he might safely venture an investment; but, recalling Dr. Hild's injunction to see the whole country before making a decision, he resolutely restrained his ardor, and took his way back to Pendleton to indulge in a few days' rest.

But his impatience hurried him on again, and he struck out northward for Wallula, purposing to make his way thence along the Snake to Walla Walla and Lewiston and over one of the mountain trails into the Big Hole of Montana.

It was late in September when he left Pendleton. The journey had been one rich in experience and in pleasure, still, he was beginning to weary a little of his mode of life. Sitting all day in the saddle, and living upon the rough fare of the wayside stations, was not just what he had pictured it in the ease of his own home. He had meant to be very candid with himself; he had expected to manage without his little elegancies; still, it was hardly to be supposed that skillets and table-cloths would have obtruded themselves far into his dream of achievement. He was a person of rather delicate tastes, rather nice sentiments; and these do not, as a rule, affiliate with bacon and brown sugar. He found himself wishing lately, with some irritation, that the waiter would bestow a little of his levity upon the biscuit, and that the tea had been born with a trifle more spirit; still, the country was like a vision, and the stomach was an inelegant organ at best.

But some way, in the ride from Pendleton to Walla Walla, Thurgar's rhapsody over the country even dropped into the minor. He had come into the alkali belt of the Columbia, and the air was hot, dry, and choking. He travelled in a cloud of dust now, so fine it sifted through his very garments, and he drank it in, in breathing, till he was on the verge of suffocation. The sun beat down with the glare of a furnace, and it seemed to the young man that he was lying in a crematory and could feel himself being slowly reduced to the same impalpable alkali.

When he reached Walla Walla, he was in sad need of rest and of recruiting. Besides, he was a little unwell, which made him the more disgusted at his situation, for the nights here were as oppressive as the days, and sleep was a wary miss not to be decoyed. He labored in vain to render his condition supportable, and finally, in despair, he set out for Lewiston. The intervening country was a stretch of barren waste, and Thurgar's heart turned yearningly to the mountains. Amid their retreats he would find rest, a healing balm, and renewed strength in their breezes. Halting, therefore, only long enough for fresh equipments, he struck out again; and in a couple of days was crossing the low surges of the foot-hills and beating up along the trail that wound into the pass. The cool breath of the frozen summits lifted his hair and played about his cheeks deliciously. He inhaled it with eagerness, and pressed along, straining up the heights for deeper draughts and a fiercer wooing. The breezes were coming now cool and stiff, but someway they did not revive him. He began to be aware of a darting pain in his head, and of sudden spells of giddiness attended by a craving for water.

The craving grew constantly till in parched desperation he turned at last from the trail and went in search of drink. A stronger attack of dizziness warned him to dismount, and, leading the horse, he made his unsteady way. He found a stream presently, for water was plenty, and drank with keen avidity. He had gone, as he judged, but a few rods from the trail, but, when he turned and retraced his steps, it had disappeared.

Hither and thither in every direction with nervous eagerness he searched, but not a trace of the vanished way. He recalled every landmark that might serve as a clue, but, alas ! the landmarks, like the path, were gone; he was lost among the mountains. Night followed day, and day followed night, and still he wandered, climbing to every new eminence in trust of a promise on the other side, but finding only in the beyond the same barren hopelessness of hills. His provisions were running low now, but, worse than all, the pain in his head had become incessant, and a low fever was wasting him. Every little while he was overtaken by weakness, when he would slip off, secure his horse, and lie down. Then, as it passed, he climbed into the saddle again.

He had continued his search through five desperate days, but on the sixth he was conscious that he could hold himself up no longer. Towards evening he was picking his way cautiously down the side of a mountain when the rein dropped from his hands. He knew he was fainting, but his strength refused to rally. He had only a memory of drawing his foot from the stirrup, of slipping a little to break the shock, and of falling. The rest was a blank; he was unconscious.

CHAPTER XXVI.

THURGAR'S next remembrance was of opening his eyes upon a gaunt, cadaverous face, framed in hair; for the thin, matted locks fell down against the man's gray beard as he leaned over, and his beard was reinforced by the hairy growth along his breast. This weird, hirsute creature was holding in his shrivelled hand a flask which he was pressing to Thurgar's lips. As the young man gazed upon the apparition, he thought vaguely that some wizard had come out of the mountain and was weaving his pernicious spell about him. It never occurred to him that a real flesh-and-blood man could be living up here amid the solitudes.

"Oh, ho! you're awake, are you?" mumbled the apparition, seeing Thurgar's opened eyes.

"Yes," said the other, faintly.

"Wall, you wuz a long time gettin' round to it. You'd better try an' pull yerself together a bit, an' git in off the hill-side. The night air's apt to be a little chilly up here in the mountings."

"Get in!" exclaimed Thurgar, in surprise. Get in where?"

He expected no less than that a chasm would suddenly yawn beside him and reveal the haunt of this musty magician deep within the granite ledge.

"Thar's the cabin," said the man, pointing down to what

time and weather had turned so brown Thurgar had failed to
distinguish it from the rocks. "'Tain't fur, nor thar ain't
no climbin'."

Thurgar made a brave effort to get upon his feet. He stood
erect a moment, but the next sank helplessly back.

His companion contemplated him. "How did you get
here, an' whar be you goin'?"

"I came on horseback, and was heading for the Big Hole;
but I lost the trail," said Thurgar, exhaustedly.

"Wall, yer cayuse must have gone on to hunt it up," with
a ghostly effort at a smile; "an' I guess you ain't likely to
foller him to-night. If you can pack yerself to the cabin
thar, 'tain't much of a place to brag on, but such as it is yer
welcome to pass the night in it."

The sight of even this weird, uncouth specimen was grate-
ful to the young man, fresh from his nightmare of wolves,
and hunger, and lonely death. He thanked him sincerely,
if faintly, for the hospitality, and once more struggled to his
feet. His companion passed an arm about the youth, and
thus slowly and cautiously they began the descent. They
had gone half over the distance, when the old man stopped.

"I've left something," he said. "I must go back."

He helped Thurgar to a seat on a large rock, and went
slowly up again. In a few minutes he returned, carrying in
his hand a large bunch of wild flowers.

"It's my son's birthday," he remarked, by way of explanation and apology.

The beautiful bright-tinted blossoms (for the flowers on

the mountain-slopes were of a gorgeous coloring) seemed yet
more vivid in contrast to the dingy quality of the old man's ap-
parel. His overalls, which had been originally of a tan, were,
like his house, weather-beaten to the dull brown of the rocks,
and hung about his shrunken legs, limp and loose. His gray
flannel shirt, which, open at the neck, left his brown breast
exposed, had outlived its beauty and largely its usefulness,
for the sleeves were wanting from the elbow, and above it
hung in a fringe of tatters about his tanned arms; while the
high gum boots, fastened to the waist by a piece of rope,
were evidently weakening at the post of service, since the
soles were held to duty under his feet by a leashing of
cord.

Thurgar surveyed the forlorn figure with a new interest,
but the old man did not appear to notice the scrutiny. He
stooped once more and helped the youth to his feet.

"What might yer name be, stranger, an' whar might you
hail from?" he asked, when they were again under way.

"I came from Eastern Washington, hunting a good stock
range. My name is Wright,—Thurgar Wright."

"Don't like yer name," he said, bluntly. "Thurgar's
good enough,—queer, but good enough; but Wright,—I
don't like it."

"I'm sorry," Thurgar replied, more in his natural defer-
ence than for any concern about the creature's likes or dis-
likes.

"But, then," the old man added, "people ain't to blame
for their names. They didn't name theirselves. Probably,

now, you won't like my name neither, for it ain't pleasant soundin'. It's Onlucky."

The name certainly was uncanny. Under most circumstances Thurgar would have been full of surmises, and might have hazarded a question; but just now his condition left no place for emotions of wonder or curiosity. His one desire was to reach the shelter of the hut and lie down.

A miner's cabin is never a thing of much structural beauty or artistic pretence; it would scarcely appeal to a domesticated eye as either commodious or ornate. Thurgar's late experience of frontier life had set the measure for his expectations here; still, nothing that he had happened upon before quite prepared him for his first glance into the interior of Onlucky's cabin.

In the corner, attached to the wall, was a bunk, over whose boards was drawn a faded comforter. Through its various rents most of the cotton wadding had worked out and disappeared, and what remained seemed trying to follow the example of the rest, for it protruded through the covering in little hummocks that looked from the door-way like patches of discolored snow. Thrown back across the foot was a blanket, thin and black from continued use, and comforter and blanket completed the outfit of the bed.

Close by, at the side of the room, stood a bare table, and behind it, against the wall, a couple of shelves were concealed by a calico curtain. These, a small sheet-iron stove, and a cracked leather satchel that had collapsed at the foot of the bunk constituted the furnishing of the cabin. But the place, in its destitute squalor, had yet an air of fantastic gentility, for the smoky walls were festooned with ferns, and bright autumn leaves were woven into scrolls across drooping branches of evergreen. One might have fancied he had strayed into some woodland dell, were it not for the rusty stove, the table, and the bunk.

"You happened along at a good time," said the miner, as he led Thurgar within. "We ain't always so fixed up, but, you see, I always lay off onct a year. Christmas and Fourth-of-Julys, an' such, ain't much account to me, but I always lay off on my boy's birthday."

"Yes?" said Thurgar.

"Lucky for you, I do, too," he added, "for the rest of the time, I've no call to go up the mounting, so I don't go."

Thurgar was paying little heed to Onlucky. He was looking at the bed. Even in his enfeebled condition, he shrank from contact with anything so uninviting. But his giddiness warned him to put away his scruples, so, with a little shiver of repulsion, he threw himself down and closed his eyes.

"Mebby you're used to a piller," said the miner, presently. He went to the satchel, opened it, and took out a worn, faded coat, whose sleeves, like those of the shirt, were missing from the elbow. He folded it together as smoothly as possible and laid it under Thurgar's head. Even this poor substitute seemed welcome, and the invalid was inwardly, if not audibly, thankful.

Meanwhile, the old man seemed to have forgotten his presence. He had brought in from somewhere outside a number of empty cans, and seated on the log stool beside the table was arranging in them the flowers he had gathered. When they were all distributed to his liking, he set the cans about the room,—some on the window-sill, others on top of the cupboard, and still others upon the table. Then he stood off beside the door and surveyed the room. He was apparently pleased with the effect, for the same ghostly smile lit up his wasted countenance.

Presently he went to the cupboard and began to engage himself with its contents. Thurgar could see him pouring out some coffee into his hand, and he was hesitating about the quantity,—stinginess and liberality dividing the impulses of his mind. He tipped down a little extra and put it back three or four times, but at last the larger sentiment prevailed, for with his hand full he went out, and, lighting a fire between two stones, set about preparing supper. Soon he was in again, arranging the things upon the table; and then the meal was ready.

"Draw up now, lad, an' have a bite to eat. You'll feel yerself ag'in when yer stomich's full," he said, rolling over the log stool and setting it in place.

Thurgar rose dizzily and made his way forward, while the old man seated himself upon the edge of the bunk. The meal, which consisted simply of bacon, potato, bread, and coffee, would scarcely have appealed to a well man as very appetizing; to Thurgar, in his weakened condition, despite his extreme hunger, it was uneatable. The bread was heavy, the coffee bitter, and his taste unaccommodating;

but with cordial hospitality the miner pressed the food upon his guest, assuring him it would " set him right up."

Seeing that even this encouragement failed to bring appetite to the stranger, he rose and went again to the cupboard. There on the top shelf was an unopened can. Onlucky looked at it long and hesitatingly. At last he reached up his bony, bronzed arm, and took it down, saying, in a tone of reflection, " I'll never see the day ag'in, an' he's somebody's lad, too."

He struck his knife into the top of the can and opened it. " Thar, now eat," he said, setting it before Thurgar. It contained some California peaches, and they seemed to the invalid at that moment the most tempting fruit he had ever beheld. He drew the can towards him, and ate greedily till he had drained even the last drop of the syrup.

" You'll feel yerself ag'in now," said Onlucky, presently, as Thurgar finished. " Them peaches struck the right spot."

Soon the intolerable pain was throbbing afresh, and Thurgar hurried back to his place upon the bed. Onlucky proceeded to clear away the remnants of the feast, and put the dishes once more in the cupboard, after which he got down his pipe and tobacco, and drew the log stool in front of the door.

For a long time he remained in silent thought, smoking quietly and gazing out into the sky. The day was fading. It crept with soft, unwearied feet up the jagged mountain-side, and leaped with delicate poise from ghostly peak to peak, pausing ever upon some aerial height to gaze again

H   15

into the vanishing world below. And softly as the day had gone the night came down. Out of the far haziness of sky, it dropped a nebulous film that drew the densities of shade from deepening voids behind. The twilight deepened into dusk, the dusk into darkness, the darkness into gloom. Then Thurgar saw the old man rise from his seat, and, standing in the door-way, stretch his thin, shrivelled hands out into the night, and call, in a voice whose defiance flickered, fainted, and melted at last into a cry of anguished entreaty,—

"O thou Onmerciful, O thou Onmerciful! spare him! spare him!"

Thurgar shivered. There was something unearthly in the action of this goulish being, standing out against the everlasting silence and solitude, invoking his pitiless deity in that weird, soul-wrung cry. It filled the youth with a vague feeling of terror, as if he had stepped into a world where the laws of human justice and mercy had no domain. And though, through the weeks that he lingered with the miner, he grew to know him in the intimacy which isolation fosters, yet every night with the same straining fascination he watched the old man as in the deepest of the gloom he stood in the door-way, stretched his wasted hands into the night, and uttered his dread, low cry. It startled Thurgar always into his first alarmed sense of malignant influences, and touched with an indefinable awe his pity for the man's unknown sorrow.

Onlucky lingered a moment on the threshold, then he came quietly in, lit an end of candle, and set about removing the decorations from the wall. The boughs of evergreen, the delicate ferns, the tinted leaves, the vivid flowers,—these that he had brought with such effort from the distant hills,—he piled them all before the cabin and set them afire. A moment they blazed; the next, they were consumed. So passed the last scene in the celebration.

When he returned to the cabin, he drew near to the bunk, expecting, evidently, to find Thurgar asleep; but the young man was awake, staring at him with his large, restless eyes.

"What ails you? can't you sleep?" Onlucky asked, abruptly.

"No; my head acts strangely, and I feel oppressed."

The miner came closer and laid his hand upon Thurgar's. Then he felt of his head and looked away with a shade of anxiety.

"What is it?" Thurgar asked, interpreting the expression.

"I'm afeard you're in for the fever."

"What fever?"

"The mounting fever. That's the way it comes on. You ain't used to livin' up so high, an' I guess it was pretty hot down thar in the Columby plains.

"I wish that cayuse had stuck by you," he continued, after a pause. "It's thirty mile to the nearest settlement. I'd think nothin' of walkin' down an' fetchin' you up a beast if I was as strong as I was onct; but I wouldn't trust myself to get down thar an' back inside of three days with these legs. They're close on to the end of their goin'. Mebbe it'll be only a little touch, though; you're young, and young things throws off a fever easier than old ones. You'd best get off the heaviest of your clothes, an' make yerself easy."

When he had done all in his power to secure Thurgar's comfort, and had administered such simple remedies as were at hand, he extinguished the candle and stretched himself upon the floor beside the bed.

"No! no!" said Thurgar, rousing himself, "you must take the bunk; at least, you must share it with me." But the old man was obstinate.

"You've a father, lad, hain't you? an' a mother?"

"Yes," Thurgar answered, but hesitatingly. Parents who could so lightly slip the leash of duty were such only in name. "Yes," he allowed.

"Then you've no call to die," said the miner, simply, and continued in his place.

All through the night, as Thurgar tossed upon his extemporized pillow, he could see through the fitful moonlight the gaunt form and the haggard face of the miner. His head was resting upon his arm, and his long, matted gray hair lay along the floor. The watcher's sympathy went out to the forlorn being, whose tenure of life, he could see, was very short.

A cloud obscured the room once, and in sudden alarm Thurgar leaned over to assure himself of the presence of the old man, for a dread haunted him of being alone. He stretched out his hand, and touched that of Onlucky, who started a little, muttered something about his boy, and turned over. Even that inarticulate speech comforted the invalid, for it relieved the oppressive silence.

By and by the day dawned. Onlucky awoke, rose quietly, and leaned across the bunk.

"Awake already? You'd better have stayed asleep," he said, shaking his head. He was troubled, but, without further remark, he lit the outside fire, and set about preparing breakfast. It was not a work of many minutes; bread and fried bacon constituted the meal,—simply this. When it was ready, he brought some to the bedside, but the young man could not eat, and a cloud passed over the miner's face as he declined.

"Mebbe you'd drink some coffee if I was to make it," he said, persuasively.

"No, water. Give me water."

Onlucky took the bucket, and Thurgar watched him going slowly down to the creek and returning. Not far from the door he stooped, and picked up the can that he had thrown out the night before. He had a vague hope that by some happy oversight a few of the peaches might have remained, but the hope was futile,—the can was empty.

All day long, Onlucky watched by the young man's side, and at night he stretched himself again on the floor. So, for the next night and the next. He was a faithful nurse, and a devoted; but, alas, devotion could not stay the insidious fever that was working its fatal way. Thurgar was growing worse; he knew that solemnly in the hours of his consciousness, which were growing now fewer and fewer.

On the morning of the fourth day the invalid had an indistinct memory of Onlucky's drawing the old coat from under his head and substituting his own good one; and of the miner's tucking the thin blanket close about his shoulders. He had wondered dimly, but glancing through the small square window he had seen that winter, a little premature because of the altitude, had set in, and that a violent storm was raging. The wind was whistling shrilly down the cañon and driving the sleet in clouds along the slopes. Thurgar closed his eyes again to shut out the dreary prospect, and fell into a troubled doze.

The same afternoon he had a dim remembrance of seeing the old man open the satchel and take out two small bags. He walked to the window, examined them long, Thurgar almost thought regretfully, and at last put them in his belt. Then Onlucky had stood looking out into the storm, and—Thurgar's memory had forsaken him.

When, towards morning, it returned, he strained over for a sight of the miner, to whom he clung now with the exacting tenacity of a child; but he did not see him. He stretched out his hand and groped everywhere, but could feel nothing. In dazed stupor he lay till the dawn enabled him to gaze about the room. There, beside his bed, were bread, bacon, and a pail of fresh water; but the old man,—he looked for him in vain,—he was gone.

CHAPTER XXVII.

In the dawn of that autumn morning, like a dismantled ship swaying and plunging before the gale, Onlucky was making his way across the spur of the mountain to the trail that led down into the valley. The storm was lashing his bent form and driving him like a hunted thing before it. But his mouth was set hard, and the light in his eyes was of a purpose that no storm could break.

The thin, straggling locks of his hair and beard, a shade the whiter for their net of snow, were tossed about on the flying gusts. The old slouch hat was drawn low over his face, and the tattered coat with its flapping fringe of sleeve was buttoned close over his hairy breast. His step was labored and feeble; still he held his course. Frequently he might be seen to pause and reel unsteadily, as though some sudden weakness had overtaken him, when he would lean his arm against a tree or a projecting ledge and rest his head upon it. Sometimes, too, he slackened his pace to break a piece from the loaf he carried in his pocket, or draw a draught from his leathern flask; but the delay was only for a moment. The next, he was hurrying on again, a mute defiance to the sweeping storm. He must not tarry, he dare not rest; these flagging energies might fail of a further response. So on and on he pressed in desperate persistence,

175

while the day wore along in that steady flow of intervals wherewith time measures alike man's joy and his extremity.

It was noon when he crossed the last divide of hills. He had left the storm behind him among the mountains, and in a calm of slumbering elements he stumbled along the trail and struck into the street of the settlement.

Men in every attitude of indolence were sitting about, listless under the drowsy sun. Conversation was desultory; there could be no urgency in speech where such an indefinite stretch of time lay before the community. Still, as the grotesque figure came up, the groups were surprised into wondering comment. But Onlucky with blind fixedness passed along, made his way into the saloon, and called for a drink.

"Come a good stretch, h'ain't ye, stranger?" inquired the loquacious bar-tender. "Ye look did up."

"No, 'tain't the distance," said the miner. "I've got past my travellin' days; that's all."

He sank into the nearest chair and leaned his head upon the table. But the table seemed suddenly unbalanced, and the room strangely undefined.

"Why, man, you're droppin'," said the other, as he hurried from behind the counter and caught the sinking figure. Two or three who had been playing at an adjoining table rushed over, and together they raised the stranger and propped him up in an angle of the window.

"Here, swaller some stiff'nin'," said the bar-keeper, pressing the liquor upon him. Onlucky lifted the glass to his lips and drained it at a draught. His upraised face was brought into distinctness against the sunshine, and with an oath one of the onlookers stepped forward.

" Wall, bless my pesky skin ef thet ain't the very same cursed, old, rantankerous Onlucky. Why, pard, I didn't know you. Give us yer hand, man,—an' how be ye, anyway? It does a feller good to see ye,—dog goned if it don't, —an' how be ye, pard? an' how in hell do ye find yerself?"

" Pretty wall, Ben, pretty wall considerin'," Onlucky replied, with the effort at cheerfulness which his miner's pride prompted.

" Come in afoot, did ye? Why, ye're played out."

" Yes," said the old man faintly, " come in to see a doctor."

" Wall, it's time ye did, pard,—high time, sure 'nough. It's a wonder ye've held out es long es ye have. I urged ye years ago to gev up thet great, barren lead an' come down among human critters, an' ye've had to come to it at last, have ye? Wall, I'm right glad to see ye. Put up the drinks, Shady, an' let ev'ry man drink his fill to the health of Onlucky; fer we're old pards, me an' him,—ay, we're old pards, fer we've knowed each other sence afore we fit the Reds together, nigh on to twenty year ago."

The bottle was pushed along, the whiskey poured, and with honest good will they drank long life to the miner; but gently, for even with their blunted perceptions the men could read the mockery of that pledge.

" I say, Onlucky," observed Unco Ben, " yer lookin' oncommon bad. Why, man, ef ye'd gev yerself any kind of a show, ye'd ought to be a-skippin' round here with the

m

youngest of us, fer ye're not a day older'n I be, I'll be bound. It's all come of stickin' by thet lead ever sence the camp bust up."

"Yes, I'm peggin' out," allowed the other. "But I've stuck by the lead so long I couldn't give it up now. It's home to me up thar, an' I reckon I'll just as well pass my checks in one place as 'nother. But I must go to the doctor now," he said, rising slowly to his feet.

"Come with me back in here an' rest a bit fust," said Unco Ben, persuasively. "Yer needin' rest. Ye look oncommon bad."

"No, friend, not now. I'm in a hurry. I want to find the doctor."

He made his way out of the door and up the street to where, over a general merchandise store, the physician of the settlement had his office. He was not within, but a man pointed him out to Onlucky where he stood leaning against a post smoking, and Onlucky walked over and addressed him.

"Thar's a lad up to the cabin that's very low with the mounting fever. I want you to come along an' fix him out."

"Wharabouts is it?" inquired the doctor, changing the pipe listlessly to the other side of his mouth.

"It's up thar to the summit, nigh on to thirty mile from here."

The doctor looked at him with a condensed surprise, which led even to the extremity of removing his pipe.

"An' ye expect me to come up thar, thirty mile, to see a

man with mounting fever? Wall, I'll be damned." He put
the pipe back in his mouth and contemplated the stranger
with a deliberateness that was chilling.

"You've got to do it; you've just got to do it," said the
miner, firmly. "He's a dyin', an' you've got to come up
straight."

The doctor laughed; it was a quiet, collected laugh.

"You'll git yer pay," said Onlucky, drawing out a bag of
dust. "I ain't askin' no favors. I'm ready to pay for the
sarvice."

The doctor's eye kindled just a trifle; still, he did not
change his expression or his attitude.

"It's a long day's ride, thar an' back, up them trails," he
remarked, slowly. "An', like's not, the feller's dead by
this, anyhow."

"No, he ain't; he can't be—dead." The doctor's misgiving was ominous; it woke a new alarm. "But," he
added, anxiously, "he soon will be if he don't get help.
Here," handing him the bag, "I was comin' this week to
lay in the winter's grub,—but a few months more of my life
ain't much value 'longside of his."

The doctor hesitated. There was a suggestion of blood-
money about this fee, and his conscience winced. But he
was not a man to be troubled with over-nice scruples, so he
took the pouch and thrust it out of sight in his pocket.

"It's too late to start to-day. I couldn't keep the trail;
but I'll be along to-morrow," he said, carelessly.

A look of deep disappointment crossed the old man's face.

"I'll give ye something to dose him with until I get thar, though," he offered, in compromise. He was unwilling to inconvenience himself, but he was ready to give such assistance as did not interfere with his comfort. He crossed to his office and prepared some powders, which he gave to Onlucky; and the latter, leaving minute directions for the doctor's guidance to the cabin, took his departure.

He turned next into the general store below, where he emptied out the contents of the other bag, and got in return a little tea and sugar, some crackers, some condensed milk, and several cans. Stowing the sugar and tea carefully in his pocket, and saving out a few of the crackers to sustain him along the way, he tied up the rest with the cans in a gunny sack which the grocer contributed, swung the sack across a knotty stick, and, with the stick upon his shoulder, struck again into the trail that led to the summit.

When in the next glimpse of the morning Thurgar turned his head and opened his heavy eyes, he seemed to see beside him on the floor, dimly outlined, a human form. With a faint cry of gladness, he called out, but no voice answered. In a hunger of longing, he summoned his strength, reached over, and touched the wasted hand. Yes, he was there, it was Onlucky, he had come back, but no motion responded to the eager touch. He was too feeble for further effort, but he lay contentedly, for he was not alone.

The day came, by and by,—a pale suffusion of light that straggled in at the little square window in blinking sleepiness. Thurgar could see the old man distinctly now. He was lying beside the bunk, face downward. One naked arm was under his head, where he had thrown it in instinctive protection when falling; the other was outstretched; and, close under his hand, as it had dropped from his helpless grasp, was the flask. His strength had failed too soon to allow him that last small swallow. The bundle lay beside him where it had rolled, and the knotted stick had fallen like a yoke across his neck. His hat was off, and the tangled gray locks still stiff with the sleet streamed down his back and lay along the floor.

As Thurgar gazed upon the prostrate figure, a fear shot through him. That man lying there on his face—was he dead? A pain, keen as a blade, went across his heart. That weird being had grown dear to his charge, and the dread of losing him froze in Thurgar all thought of his own condition, and he cried aloud and gathered all his force and called again and again.

At last the old man turned his head a little, feebly, confusedly. "Yes, lad, yes, I'm a-comin'. It's a long ways, a fearful ways; but I'm a-comin', I'm a-comin'."

His mind was clouded. He was living over in fancy that terrible walk from the settlement. There was a long silence, then, supporting himself upon his elbow, Onlucky passed his free hand again and again over his forehead. His thoughts were regaining distinctness, for he reached out to the bacon that remained untouched, and commenced eating voraciously, swallowing great gulps of water as he ate. The food revived

16

him, and presently with an effort he crawled up to the bunk
and leaned over.

"Cheer up, lad," he said, with his ghastly smile; "cheer
up. I've been to the valley to fetch you some medicine, an'
the doctor'll be along now to straighten you out. I brought
a supply of them peaches, too, to see if we couldn't coax up
a little appetite."

Thurgar could only press in his the gnarled hand, but a
drop like a tear stood in Onlucky's eyes as he turned away.
He hastened to draw from his belt the prescribed powder,
and to administer it as the doctor had directed; then he lay
down beside the bunk again, waiting, and was overjoyed to
see presently that Thurgar had fallen into a doze. He
dropped asleep himself soon, unconsciously, from exhaustion, and in the cabin all was quiet, till along towards noon
they were both aroused by the sound of a voice hallooing
outside. It required several attempts to get Onlucky to his
feet, and the hallooing had broken into a good round oath
before he succeeded in making his way across the room and
opening the door.

CHAPTER XXVIII.

It was the doctor sitting comfortably astride of his horse, waking the echoes of a hundred cliffs with his din. The wretched aspect of Onlucky, as he drew himself forward through the snow to welcome his visitor, modified somewhat the latter's wrath at the delay, and his tone was lowered to reasonable civility as he accosted the miner.

"This is a despret lonesome spot ye've chose for a residence," he observed, as he dismounted. "Why, I ain't struck a cabin sence I left the settlemint."

"No, thar ain't much prospectin' any more along this creek."

He led the way into the cabin, to the bunk where Thurgar lay. The youth was alive yet, and fortunately conscious. The physician counted the pulse, noted the temperature, and shook his head. He was not addicted to the delicacy of concealing his opinions. The patient was low,—too low to warrant any hope, though in life there was, of course, always a chance. In support of the chance, he would add his effort, and see if native vigor might yet foil the disease. He detailed minutely the treatment necessary, and then, being quit of his mission, he fortified himself in a hearty repast and prepared to return. He had mounted, when in some sudden after-thought, he dismounted again, handed the bridle to Onlucky, returned to the cabin and leaned over the bunk.

" Say, chap, ye 'wake ?"

Thurgar nodded feebly.

" Wall, if ye live, ye'd better set up the old man, or he'll snuff out this winter. He's gev me the last of his dust."

Then, having relieved his mind of any possible responsibility in the transaction, he mounted once more and rode away.

A long contest was this in the lonely cabin on the Bitter Root,—a delusive contest against fateful odds. Autumn had gone. No longer the sun struck his steely gleams from the sharp faces of the rock; no longer the shimmer of the valley left them suspended between two skies. The snow had spread over all its white deception, and winter sat upon the peaks, cold and austere. These were dark days to the two, snowed in on the borders of the habitable. To Thurgar, in his delirium, it seemed, when the great gusts tore along the mountain-side, swirling the snow eddies across the chasms, that the spiritual agencies within him had materialized, and were sweeping cabin and men together to that chill outer world of death. But nature was kinder than his thought; the winds passed by, bearing to the spectral kingdom, not a human soul, but only the veiled presence that had waited by the door.

Faithfully, ceaselessly Onlucky had tended his charge. His energy was the hostage that walk to the settlement had exacted, and he could never ransom it now, but his poor remnant of strength was freely expended. And his reward was vouchsafed him, for a day came at last when Thurgar could be propped up in the bunk and rejoice the heart of the miner with his relish of the peaches.

The heavy fall of snow which barred all hope of escape from the cabin had committed Thurgar to a compulsory recruiting, so he was well along to recovery when one morning a chinook swept up, bringing in a transient spring-time on its breath. The winter loosened his rigid grasp, and the snow, a fickle favorite, opened her arms to the dallying breeze and was transformed into a thousand little brooklets that mocked her discomfiture as they sped away.

Onlucky had rolled the seat out before the door, and sat smoking quietly and gazing along the recovered vista of the valley. Thurgar came out and leaned irresolutely against the hut. He was anxious to avail himself of an opportunity so favorable to his need, yet loath to take leave of the old man. Some kindred emotion advised Onlucky of the rival impulses, for he said, bluntly,—

"You think it's time you was makin' a break for home, eh, lad?"

"Yes, I've been indebted to you a long time, and for more than I can ever repay. I must not increase the debt by remaining longer."

"It will be lonesome up here now, when you're gone." The remark was one of soliloquy rather than of address. "But, then, it won't be for long, I'm thinkin'."

"No, it can't be for long." Thurgar drew near and laid his hand on the miner's shoulder.

16*

"You're not long for this world, Onlucky, and I wish you'd be persuaded to come back with me to my home. I'm rich,—that is, I will be,—and nothing could be more of a pleasure than to cherish, to its latest, the life that rescued mine."

"I thank you, lad, for the offer." The voice was a little unsteady. "It 'ud be a priv'lege to me, sure 'nough, to be near you, but I'm not fit to live in the world now. It 'ud be strange to me, an' I'd be strange to it."

"No, no; you shall have a little spot all alone, where no one shall intrude but myself. Do, Onlucky, let me feel that I can, at least in small measure, return your devotion."

"I couldn't," said the old man, shaking his head positively. "I've lived here nigh on to twenty year, an' here I'll die."

Thurgar knew, by the tone, that the resolution was inflexible. "Then, at least, you will let me provide for you. Remember, you gave your last dust to the doctor."

Onlucky glanced up sharply. How had he come by that information?

"He told me himself," said Thurgar, in answer to the glance. "You've nothing to last out the winter. Come, at least you will share my money."

But the old man shook his head more persistently than before. "I don't want yer money," he said, with dignity.

"But, Onlucky, my friend, what will you let me do? I cannot leave you this way; you will not condemn me to the humiliation of taking everything and giving nothing."

The old man looked up at him. A sudden eagerness

spoke from the wan, wasted face, and flashed in the two
piercing eyes.

" Do you want, earnest and solemn, to repay me ?"

" Yes, indeed."

" Then I'll tell you how you can do it."

He leaned forward and grasped the young man's arm.
" Give me a bit of yer strength. I've saved it; give me a bit
of yer strength."

" What do you mean, Onlucky,—a bit of my strength ?"

" Yes, give me a month of yer work yon'er in the tunnel.
Four weeks more ef us two workin' 'll fetch us in whar the
lead must be if she's thar. Let me know the truth about the
lead, an' I'm ready to die."

He kept his hand locked grimly about Thurgar's arm,
awaiting his reply.

" A month or a year," he answered, heartily ; " I shall work
till you are satisfied."

The old man relaxed his grip ; his excitement was visible
in the tremor that shook his frame.

" You're the right sort of stuff, lad," he said, at last. " I
was afeard mebbe you was above workin' with yer hands, for
I can see you've been raised gentle. But you won't dig for
nuthin'. If we strike anything, I'll go shares with you, half
an' half; an' I only ask one month. If we don't come on
till anything by that, you can go, an' we'll call it all squar'."

A few minutes later Thurgar Wright might be seen
emerging from the cabin. His coat and vest had been discarded; the sleeves of his blue-flannel travelling shirt were

rolled up above the elbow, and left bare his white, shapely arms. In his hand he carried a candle, and across his shoulder, a pick and a shovel. He walked quickly down the narrow trail that led to the creek; and after him, with a more halting step, came the decrepit form of the miner.

CHAPTER XXIX.

IT was distressing to Thurgar to watch the concentrated energy that spent, old man hurled into the blows of his pick, through those days when they tunnelled together into the iron mountain. It was his last chance, his last hope. The lead, to which he had committed his life, on which he had exhausted his years, was it barren or productive? He must throw in the remnant of his strength, and know now. In vain Thurgar pleaded with him to desist, assuring him that he would not leave, however long the labor, till the lead was thoroughly proved; Onlucky was obstinate. To have the desire of his heart gratified at last, filled him with too much impatience to admit of idleness. So, side by side they wrought in the dim passage, while the sharp strokes in weakening echoes rang along the jagged walls and died out in the distant darkness.

Every little while Onlucky lowered his pick, and leaned against the side-face for support; but in a minute he was erect again, dealing his terrific blows upon the stubborn rock. This desperate eagerness to reach the lead filled Thurgar with an aching pity. What of good could the ore contribute though it were of fabulous richness? The miner's life could be counted in days, he knew; and every night, when the young fellow stretched himself upon the floor where before

189

the other had lain, he had a dim foreboding that the morning would find Onlucky past all solicitude for his lead. But dawn still saw the miner on his feet, laboring with the same feverish force.

And Thurgar, for his pity and his love, outdid Onlucky. There was no hoarding of strength, but fiercely, recklessly he strove, as though his own hope too was staked on this perilous issue. They were riding a race with death, here in the dim, narrow tunnel, and he struck every blow for victory. They made rapid progress; they were eating right into the heart of the granite mountain; but the days lengthened into weeks, and the weeks passed,—one, two, three, four,—and they had found no trace of the expected lead.

As they returned along the trail to the cabin, that last evening of the allotted month, the silence was unbroken, for the old man spoke not a word. He sat later than usual by the fire, and his prayer that night was faint and faltering. Before he extinguished the candle, he set out breakfast upon the table, the best that his little stock afforded; then throwing himself upon the bunk, he said quietly,—

"Make an early start, lad, so's you'll have plenty of time. Keep the left-han' trail, all the way down; an' now—good-by."

He extended his hand, and clasped Thurgar's lingeringly a moment. Then he turned over in the bunk, and went calmly asleep.

What time in the night or early morning the young man arose, Onlucky could not tell, but when he awoke, Thurgar was gone. The condition of the table showed that he had eaten his breakfast, and Onlucky smiled faintly as he noted that, to the last, the peaches had held their relish.

He did not hurry to rise this morning; there was nothing to rise for any longer. All hope of the lead was gone; he had made his final effort and had failed,—"Onlucky" all the way, for, to the end, fate had baffled him. He did not think of digging further; they had got to where the lead should be, and it was not there; that was all.

The strain was over, and he was paying the penalty of all forced action. He was exhausted, spent, and he knew that the weakness was but the slow approach of dissolution. And yet he did not quail, this strange, hope-reft man, alone in the voiceless waste. What was death? What of bitterness or of desolation could it hold that his life had not known? Was there a future? He did not know. Was there a God? He did not care much. If there was, he had encountered him in only one evidence, retribution; and the retribution of eternity might increase in duration, it could not in degree, what he had known already. The one absorbing wish to which he had narrowed desire, which had seemed to hold an inevitable promise of fulfilment,—that, too, had proved a cheat. To the last, to the very last, vengeance had followed him.

The morning sun crept across the smoky window, and circled slowly around, trailing its brightness farther and farther from the cabin. It slanted in at the abandoned shaft, and peered about with a mocking curiosity. It lit up the windlass, and crept across the dump of grayish waste as though measuring off in the pile the years of the old man's folly. It lent to every familiar object a moment of vivid distinctness, then slipped away: Onlucky and his belongings were passing together into the shadow.

The vertical noontide dropped between the hills, and lay along the valley. From his bunk Onlucky could not look into its bosom, but he knew that down below there the little creek was hurrying off from the tunnel, and that the sunbeams were stealing stealthily over the unsightly cavern.

As he watched the light creeping back out of the valley, the long, distant shadows told him that the afternoon had gone, and that the day was near its close. Still he held his listless posture on the bunk. The day had been long and dreary: why should he rise to watch its fading? Through the dingy square he could see the cold, rigid mountains. What were they but white monuments of death?—death! The earth was full of it; time fed upon it; eternity was rooted in it. And this mellow light of the dying day, that lit up the sepulchral peaks with a glory as of a holy promise,— this, like the rest, was delusive. There was no promise in its radiance,—nothing but deception. It would fail in a moment now, and the world would settle into darkness. But suddenly, as if in denial, right across the cabin floor lay a long beam of sunlight. He started a little, but he did not move. Then full across the sunshine fell the shadowed outline of a man. He turned and leaped up. There in the door-way Thurgar Wright was standing; his attitude was one of suppressed excitement.

"Why, lad, my lad," cried the miner, springing towards him, "what's happened? You sick agen, that you've come back?"

"Come back!" said Thurgar, with a sly smile. "Why, man, I haven't gone yet."

He stepped quickly across the room and laid upon the table a handkerchief in which were wrapped five or six samples of rock. "We've struck the lead, Onlucky, and that's what we've got," he said, simply.

For a moment the miner stood spellbound. Then, with the rapidity of lightning, he shot forward, seized a specimen, and darted through the door. He looked at it searchingly, he tasted it, scraped it with his nail, struck off a piece against the rocky ground, scraped again, looked closer; then the gleam of a joy unutterable flashed into his ashen face, he stretched aloft his shrivelled hand, and from his lips broke a cry, wild and quivering, "At last! at last! Gold! gold! gold!"

Thurgar was beside him in an instant; and together the two men stood, locked in each other's arms. Then Onlucky stepped back, and, standing again in the door-way, with the light of the setting sun falling upon his old head like a benediction, he stretched his tremulous hands up to the still, white peaks, and called, brokenly,—

"God! God! you're th' Onmerciful no longer, for you've spared him,—you've spared him."

He bowed his head, and tears rolled slowly down and dropped upon the ore, but, brushing them quickly away, he turned, and came quietly back into the house. He threw himself again upon the bed, and said, in a tone of wonderful calmness,—

"I'm ready to go now, lad, an' glad to go, for my boy'll be rich,—how rich you don't suspicion, for you don't know the fortune you've struck in them rocks."

The proving of the lead and the finding of the treasure would have inspired most men with a desire to live; it only filled Onlucky with a readiness for death. IIis life began to ebb almost perceptibly, and their positions became reversed, for Thurgar was watching with the old man. In the evening of the next day the miner called his companion.

"The time's a-most up, lad," he said, quietly, "an' I want to know, afore I go, that you'll do with the mine as I d'rect you. I'm leavin' you a charge as 'ud be a temptation to most men, for that mine's got more 'n one fortune in it; but I know it won't tempt you. You'll see my will carried out, won't you?"

"Yes," said Thurgar, and the solemnity of his tone lent to the word the sanctity of an oath.

"Then set down on the stool thar, an' pay careful heed to me."

He was lying on the bunk, but, rising, he went over to the old satchel and returned with two papers.

"This here," he said, seating himself, and spreading out the first upon the bed, "is a deed to your half the mine. I said I'd d'vide, an' now you have it."

IIe passed his eye rapidly over the document, and folding it again placed it on the table beside Thurgar.

"An' this," he said, taking up the remaining document, "is the deed to th' other half. I've made a will d'vidin' it atween two persons, the unly two in the world that b'long to me,—an' they don't b'long to me nuther, I suppose."

Thurgar wondered a little at the paradox, but he did not question. It belonged with Onlucky's private sorrow, which was sacred against his intrusion.

"To put you in the way of trackin' 'em," he continued, reflectively, "I'll have to go back, way back, till when I was a lad unly a little older 'n you be yerself. It's the hist'ry of my life, but you'll have to know it. It's been my secret, an' now it's got to be yours; an' 'member, lad, if you're ever tempted to use it agen me, that an ole man, when he was helpless, trusted you."

He spoke very slowly. The exertion of speech was wearing, and he paused frequently for rest, and to control his breath. He passed his hand three or four times across his forehead now, as though straightening out his thoughts, and commenced his recital.

"I was a chap somewheres about your age, when I met a girl that I loved an' she loved me. I'd never knowed any love all my life, for I'd no father nor mother, an' I'd been knocked about the world doin' for myself 's long 's I ever knowed anythin' about it. But I'd a pile of ambition in them days, an' I was smart too, people said; leastwise, I was sober an' honest, an' them count a heap towards helpin' a feller along. Little by little I worked ahead till I got a place in a bank. This was in Portland, a little town down on the

Willamette in Oregon. I've heerd say it's growed to be quite a place, an' we all reckoned it must, in them days."

"Yes, it's a large town," said Thurgar. "I know it very well. I ought to."

"Them towns all growed fast when they got a start. That place hadn't no more 'n three hundred people when I fust come and settled thar. Wall, I saw the girl and loved her, —how much I won't try t' tell you, for, lad, if you ever love a girl as I loved that un, you'll know words jest don't mean nothin' for tellin' it. She was rich, but she didn't sot much store by money, an' we was livin' along lookin' forred to the time we'd be together in the little cot, for I was a buildin' it at odd times. I was a likely lad in them days. You wouldn't think it from this ole wreck you see left. But it ain't age has wore me out. Besides, you can't jedge of a man by what you fin' of him survivin' twenty year of camp life, an' roughin' it alone in the Rockies. Thar don't much remain, but jest the life in his body, that's the same. But I was a likely lad then, and we was to be married shortly."

He leaned his arms upon the table, and looked away in silence. A dull wistfulness settled into the keen, gray eyes, and the thin lips softened; he was lost in a gentle revery.

"He was a queer man, that ole father of hers," he remarked, abruptly. "He'd been a pi'neer, an' saw hard times, an' he'd sot his face like a flint agen his children marryin' poor. Besides, for some reason (I never knowed what), he was sot agen me from the first. It was uphill work, my courtin', lad, but she'd a faithful heart, that girl, and she knowed she was more'n my life to me; so we'd sot the day, an' I'd the little place all fixed up ready to fotch her home. Then the ole man died,—yes, died, an' died,— biddin' her leave me."

He rose and began to pace the floor, muttering incoherently. His foe seemed to grow into a visible presence, which he addressed with ever-growing bitterness. His spasmodic gestures had a threatening import, and the long locks about his head lent wolfish suggestions.

"Oh, lad!" he broke out, recalling for a moment his guest, "may you never have call t' hate a human bein' as from that hour I've hated that man. He's never rested in his coffin. He couldn't, for my hate has moved his bones ev'ry hour he's laid thar." His eyes were gleaming like two balls of fire, and his face, as it looked out from the circle of matted hair, was livid in its anger. A shudder passed over Thurgar. It was a fearful thing to see this vindictive being carrying down into eternity such relentless hatred of his youth's enemy. Yet could he blame him? In Thurgar's heart was an enforced fellow-feeling; he knew he too would have hated that father.

There was a silence, in which every power of the old man's soul seemed up in conflict. He had waged a long fight with this foeman, but he was ready now to hurl his last breath into a final close.

Thurgar saw that in the spiritual grapple Onlucky's life was ebbing. "But the girl," he said, rising quickly, and

17*

standing before him, " this girl that you loved so! She loved you, you said, and was going to marry you?"

" Eh! What!" he gasped. " The girl that loved me, that I was goin' to marry,—yes, the girl! the girl!"

His foe was forgotten, but still he paced the floor,—slowly now, to and fro, muttering drearily, " the girl, yes, the girl!

" I knowed somethin' was goin' to happen," he said, at last, lifting his desolate eyes to Thurgar's. " I felt it all about me,—a great blackness of fearin' that I'd lose her. An' I did lose her," he cried, brokenly. " She come one night when I was waitin' for her down by the river, an' she told me it was all up atween us; she would never be my wife.

" I went crazy that night, lad," he said hoarsely, glaring in Thurgar's face, " crazy, crazy, for I took her home to the little house, an'—an'——" He leaned far over the table, and whispered huskily, " I betrayed her. Yes, lad,—the girl I loved,—I betrayed her."

He put both his hands to his head, and, sinking back, buried his face against the bed. To Thurgar the revelation was too terrible. He could only gaze at the motionless figure in a horrified silence. The crouching form, the averted face, they told to the fullest in what a torment of expiation this convict of memory had passed his years. His crime had been great; how fearfully he had atoned!

The story, as it struck upon Thurgar's mind, was set in all its heinous repulsiveness. He seemed to have turned his face against a pit whose blackness was impenetrable to eyes adjusted only to purity. Unconsciously he drew back as though fearful of some hideous contagion, but as he watched the miner, gradually pity for the man overcame repulsion for the criminal, and he laid his hand gently upon his companion's shoulder. Onlucky raised his head with a look of gratitude at the silent sympathy, and slowly he drew himself erect again.

"My story's a'most done now, lad," he said. "You draw away from me, and so you may. Thar's no crime a man can carry on his soul so black as that un. I've never saw an outcast woman, but I've said in my heart, 'first of all, some wretch like me betrayed her,' an' I've never saw a man goin' headlong to the devil but I've thought, 'he's buryin' some shame.' I've never b'lieved in no God like other folks, but thar's been a vengeance huntin' me ever sence. Thar wasn't no need for God's vengeance, though," he said, drearily; "I'd 'nough in my own heart. If I hadn't loved her, 'twouldn't have been so hard, but, lad, I loved her double for the thought of how I'd wronged her.

"She spoke to me jest onct sence that night," he continued, after a pause; "that was months after. She'd gone with her sister down to 'Frisco, they'd gev out, an' I knowed, of course, what 'twas about. They was gone a long time, an' one day it come over me all of a suddint, an idee that they hadn't gone thar at all. I sot out quick over to the ranch her father'd left her; an' thar, sure 'nough, I see the smoke a-curlin' out of the chimbly. It was along in the fall, an' the rains was drenchin' me, an' I was wore out fastin'; but I crept up closer an' closer, until I got under the winder, an' I sot down. Thar wasn't no one thar but the girl an' her sister,—for I heerd unly them two voices all the time I was waitin'. Wall, the second night, as I was sittin' thar, I heerd a great hurryin' in the room, an' a shuttin' of doors an' a low moanin'. I stood up an' listened. The moanin' went on for hours, an' then I heerd three, four cries, that'll sound deep down in my grave, I know. Then everythin' was still again. By an' by I caught the little, low cry of a baby, an', lad, all the power on earth couldn't have kept me when I heerd that baby's voice. It drawed me right along, so God Almighty's self couldn't have held me back. I walked to the door, opened it, an' stood inside.

"Thar she lay, with her bright yellow hair all over the bed, an' on her arm, my child,—yes, lad, my child. I stud like fixed. She saw me an' half raised herself, an' the look of hate that come into her face, I'll never, never forget it. All the love was gone. She drawed the little un close to her bosom as if she was unwillin' my sight 'ud even rest on it, an' I knowed I was shut out from them both forever. Ah, God! how I yearned to rush over an' clasp that girl in my arms an' claim that little un. She was a mother, an' yet as pure 's an angel in heaven, an' as beautiful. I never knowed how a human critter could long for anythin' till I see that woman with that child agen her breast. But I never moved from the spot whar I stud. The hate in her eyes held me right thar, and, when at last she raised her hand, I felt God's sentence must be light 'longside of hers.

"'Go!' she said to me. 'In life an' in death, I an' my

child, let us never look upon your face agen.' An' I turned, opened the door, an' went back into the rain."

He was silent, his locked fingers were buried between his knees, and his head was bent as though the hand of judgment hung above it still. For a long time he did not speak; the memory of his banishment froze his further thoughts, and Thurgar, too, was mute in the presence of that doom.

"I went back to my ole place an' waited," he said, finally. "I felt I must know what was to be done with that child. In a month they come home, an' then I knowed. It wasn't mine, an' it wasn't hers: it was her sister's. That woman that I hated worse 'n her ole father, even,—she had my boy,—she had my boy."

He bowed his head upon his breast and sobbed aloud, and softly down Thurgar's cheeks flowed the tears of a fervid compassion. He loved this old, forsaken creature, and he forgot the sin in the suffering.

"I couldn't bear it," Onlucky faltered. "I jest couldn't bear it; an' I went home, shet myself up in the little house, an' sot it afire. It was a coward's death, but I didn't care for that, so's I could die; but, lad," he said, looking up nervously in Thurgar's face, "when the fire was a roarin' an' a cracklin' aroun' me, I heerd that baby's voice agen. It was a-callin' an' a-drawin' me jest as it did afore. I fought it back, I shet my teeth and jumped forred to the flames, but it called an' called; an' at last, with a great yell, I leaped through the winder an' follered it. Along the path, through the woods, all the way to the house I run like mad, but when

I come thar, everythin' was still; the little un was done
callin'.

"The child had bid me live; my home was gone; so I
jest struck out across the country, found a squad goin' in
afoot to the mines, an' I've been here ever sence.

"That boy,—he's never been out of my heart an hour,"
he said, in a tone of wonderful tenderness. "An' yet I'd be
glad you'd find him dead. It's a terrible thing for a child
to have no father; though mine'll never know it; she saved
him that. I've worked for him day and night. I wanted to
leave him rich so's the time 'ud never come when his love
'ud be tore from him like mine because he was poor. I
tried to get the money gamblin' sometimes, but luck was
agen me. That was all I ever wished, to leave him rich,—
that an' one thing else,—oh! lad, to see him,—for one moment to look upon my son (he's a growed man, like you, by
this),—to look upon my son,—that he'd read in my face how
his wretched father had loved him, an' that I might cotch in
his young eyes one passin' gleam of fergivin'—oh, lad, lad,
I'd give my life for one sight of my boy,—but in life—an'
in death I must never—look—upon his—face."

As he repeated the words of his awful sentence, he tottered
and fell heavily forward against the table. The strain of his
recital had drained his vital force, and he was sinking.

To Thurgar Onlucky's sentence seemed intolerably severe;
he had been punished out of all proportion to his sin. He
hated the tyrant who had decreed the evil. He condemned
the woman as vindictive; she had been harsh, cruel; she

should have shown mercy, she should have pitied. True, she had been wronged irreparably, but then—she was unknown to Thurgar; he entertained for her no personal feeling. He was alive to her disgrace, but there was nothing to make him her partisan, and with the charitable indulgence of prejudice he was ready to condone an offence that affected only a stranger. He put out his hand to help the miner back to the bunk, but the old man's eye fell upon the folded paper, and, straightening himself with slow effort, he reached over and drew it to him.

"You know my story now, lad," he said. "I've made my will, leavin' the mine to them two. You must hunt till you find 'em. You will find 'em, for their names was knowed an' they was honest ones. But look you, lad," he called, huskily, grasping Thurgar's arm as in a vice, "if you tell my boy I was his father,—if you tell my boy I—was—his—father,—I'll curse you—with a curse—that is deeper 'n—hell."

He staggered back a step in the recoil of his own intense feeling, and Thurgar turned his head away in pained affront at the unworthy doubt. Onlucky perceived the attitude of wounded dignity, and in quick, repentant affection laid his hand down upon Thurgar's.

"Thar's the document, lad," he said. "Track 'em till you find 'em, for like 'nough they've moved away long 'go. When you do find 'em, say nothing to the boy,—his outcast father can send no message to him; but tell her, the mother, that to the last Allan Brong loved her."

"Allan Brong!" Thurgar bounded forward. "Allan Brong! And the names of the others?"

There was no shaded pity in the tone now; it was harsh, discordant: the words struck across the air with a rasp. The sin had lost its venial quality and had taken on the deadly aspect of a personal relationship. "The names of the others?" he called.

"The boy's last name was the same 's yours. They called him Edgar Arthur Wright, an' the girl was Jean Fennimore."

"Villain!" broke like a clap of thunder from the young man's lips. "Villain! Wretch! that girl was—my mother."

The blow that he struck as he spoke was charged with all the strength of his rage, and it hurled the old man across the room, where he lay against the wall, insensible. Thurgar did not move. The anger, the injured, outraged fierceness that filled his breast was too keen for pity; the bitter, resentful fury had no place for mercy,—the wrong was too deep—too deep. He looked down on the inanimate form without a sense that he had meted out anything but justice. Life was extinct, he thought. The blow had a fatal purpose, and a fatal force he knew, and, in the first surge of resentment, no remorse pleaded a gentler judgment for the dead.

But the insensible form seemed struggling inwardly. Some deathless faculty, refusing its release, still clung to the sodden clay. Some power stronger than death itself was forcing the spirit back to life. His wonderful will was holding the spectre off, and fighting its way from the threshold of eternity down into time again. A tremor passed over the shrunken form,—a shudder of nerves recalled to a finished task, a fluttering of pulses that had ceased to beat. The purpose of his soul was shaking consciousness from its torpor, and setting thought to its work again. The hands twitched a little mechanically, as though for a motor duty they had failed to understand. But gradually the straining will drew the fibres into action. The body straightened; the head, weak, unsteady, got poise upon the neck. Then, groping with his palsied hands about the mud-lined wall, he braced himself and struggled to his feet,—but blindly, for his eyes were set. An inner force of sight and impulse was urging him forward, and slowly, dazedly he tottered across the room, and, standing close, turned his vacant eyes against Thurgar's.

The fearful struggle of resurrection awoke in the youth tempestuous emotions, but they swayed him only to inactivity. The revelation had brought a stinging sense of dishonor which had avenged itself in that unmeditated blow; but the tense moments in which the miner was wresting himself from death shook in Thurgar cords not yet dead to vibration. This was the man who had saved his life, who had tended, who had loved him, whom he had loved. In the drawn, ashen face was a something that recalled the tremulous "O thou Onmerciful! spare him! spare him!" and in the dazed expression was the same wistful blank that had echoed in his "It's a long ways, lad, a fearful ways; but I'm a-comin', I'm a-comin'."

18

As Thurgar looked into the vacant eyes there was a fluttering instinct of pity, a regret, an impulse almost of protection.　He moved to support the reeling form, but the tender
purpose passed, for into Onlucky's upraised countenance the
light of intelligence came back, the brief oblivion was blotted
out, and the two stood face to face in the naked presence of
a living memory.　In the old man's gaze was no resentment,
no reproach, only a hunger, a longing, a frail hope bridging
a great gulf of despair.

"Her son? Jean's son?" he gasped, in a whisper.　"No,
it can't be! It can't be!"

He looked closer.

"Her son? Jean's son?" He fixed his gaze full upon
Thurgar's.　"Jean's son? Jean's son? Oh, God! oh, God!
yes,—the same hate in the eyes. He is Jean's son. He is
Jean's son!"

He sank upon the bed, silent, motionless.　No word of
protest, no voice of entreaty; only a look riveted upon Thurgar, the look of a love unutterable.

Feebly Onlucky raised his arms and stretched them out.
The yearning of a lifetime spoke in that mute appeal.
Faintly he moved his lips, but the tremulous cry, "My boy!
my boy!" by some mystery of power thrilled down into
Thurgar's soul.　As, long before, the voice of the child had
smote the heart of the father, so now the father's anguished
call quivered deep in the heart of the son. It drew him with
its subtle strength; it conquered him. The sin, the guilt,
the shame, the wrong,—they were all forgiven, they were

all forgot; and, with a low sob of "Father!" Thurgar was buried on the old man's breast. Only an instant of joy, only a breath of peace; for, when Thurgar raised his head and looked in his father's face, Allan Brong was dead.

CHAPTER XXX.

It was mid-afternoon of a January day that Thurgar Wright leaned against the railing of the little river steamer that puffed its way across the Columbia and vanished amid the verdure of the lower Willamette. It was headed for Portland, and Thurgar was nearing home.

The rain had fallen steadily since he crossed the mountains in the dull persistence of the season's duty. It ceased now for a time, but the landscape was only the drearier. The sky was heavy, the river dark and swollen. No rainbow bridged the rocks to halo the leaping rill, no bird shook out his rapture from sun-swept bower of leaves. There was no sheen to-day on pearly cascades astern, no gleaming light flashed back from waves that shoaled to the shore. The trees with drooping heads sat brooding on the bank, and there to the east Hood had withdrawn behind his mottled veil. The mist caught up the distance with all its fair illusions and left only a sombre prospect of forest, of turgid stream, of grim and sullen hills.

Yet this was the same scene that had smiled upon his going; that had waved its 'bon voyage' from every peak and every leaf that tossed above the river. How changed it was now. But was he himself the same? Had he not left behind a something of his identity in those wild, unpeopled

Rockies? He was missing his youth, the free, careless merriment that would never come again.

He wondered as he recalled that autumn morning that he had felt no presentiment of what he was going forth to meet; that all unwarned he had left this spot where his mother had lived out her sorrow, where the tragedy of his own being had been enacted and buried, and had gone away to the desolation of those far off mountains to learn the history of his disgrace. Everything was explained to him now,—his mother's anxiety, her lurking fear; he could understand her marriage and her persistent refusal of Emory Hild. It was all plain at last, she had kept her secret faithfully; she too had " spared him." He sighed wearily. There was nothing to spare him now. Nothing! Yes, there was much; he felt it the instant the word was uttered. He would not have this fact of his birth given to the world. He shrank repugnantly from the thought that any one but himself should know it, and yet—and yet—there was a struggle in the young heart. It showed in every feature of his handsome face; but when the gang-plank was lowered, and Thurgar stepped across it to the wharf, though the curve still lingered in the sensitive mouth and the open brow was clouded, the large dark eyes were clear.

He walked briskly along the business street, and springing nervously up the steps entered Dr. Hild's apartments. In the outer room several people were awaiting their turn for consultation; he passed through them, and giving a hasty knock stood within the private office.

"Well, Thurgar, boy," said the doctor, rising with out-stretched hand, "you have got home at last. Where in the realms of space—but—what is the matter?"

His quick eye had read in the expressive face that something was amiss, and his tone was low and anxious.

"Attend yourself, Selim, to the patients," Thurgar remarked to the assistant, "or dismiss them. I want to see Dr. Hild alone."

The assistant went out, and they stood side by side,—Emory Hild and the man who had come to tell of his own dishonor. But he did not flinch, and only the occasional twitching of the lip betrayed at what cost he was speaking. He related the story as it had been related to him; told of the awful recognition when Allen Brong had given the names of himself and Jean Fennimore, of how he had struck the guilty man, and how at last they had been united. He told it all without reserve or favor to his feelings, and, when it was done, he stood still, but his eyes were fixed upon the face opposite to him.

The doctor was standing impenetrable, as he had stood ever since Thurgar had begun his revelation. What he was thinking the young man could not know; but his keen mind, morbidly acute and sensitive now, was leaping fast to a conclusion. This man, to whom he had humbled himself, whom he had made partaker of his secret, whom he had trusted,—this man was silent. Thurgar stepped in front of him; his eyes had the glint of steel, his breath was coming quick and hot, and his fine mouth was cruel.

The doctor glanced up in calm, collected mein, and met the other's threatening gaze.

"You condemn her?" he gasped, hoarsely: "you condemn —my mother?"

The question began in a challenge, but it ended almost in a sob. The resentment was overborne by the crushing force of pain and humiliation. The passionate heart had outleaped to meet a generous sympathy: instead, there was not a word, and he drew away. Emory Hild was shaken from his self-absorption. He had caught half unconsciously the accusation in the tone, but the movement of withdrawal and the keen disappointment in the face struck the charge back vividly across his thought. He laid his strong hand softly as a woman upon the boy's head.

"Condemn her, Thurgar? Jean, my Jean?" In an instant he had caught up his hat, and was down into the street; and Thurgar, darting after him, followed at quickest speed. The young man was an athlete and a scientific walker, but he would have been a champion who had kept abreast of Emory Hild that day.

A queer pair they made, passing along the street,—the large, stately figure of the doctor, and close behind him the youth, tanned, unshorn, clay-stained, and ragged, just as he had stepped out of the tunnel up in the distant Bitter Root. Many a passer stopped, stared, turned, and stared again, in-credulous that these two could really be the distinguished Dr. Hild and Thurgar Wright, the handsome heir of the banker. But neither paused by the wayside for courtesies.

As they bounded up the marble steps, Emory Hild drew

back : here he must wait for admittance. But Thurgar threw wide the door, and they entered together. Up the velvet-lined stairs, straight to the little parlor where the boy's instinct told him he should find his " aunt." Then he paused and opened the door softly.

All through her life there had been to Jean a conviction—it was part of the mysterious knowledge which comes to every human soul—that some time, somewhere she must stand undisguised, must face the past, and see the veil lifted from her life's tragedy. How, when, she might not tell ; but in the " to be," grim, inexorable, was waiting Fate. To-day the sombre mists brought vague foreboding. She was standing beside the window looking out across the town to the distant hills. The peaks had a dreary chillness ; the clouds were folding down oppressive palls. She turned ; they were standing before her,—Thurgar and Dr. Hild. A glance,—only that,—but she knew that the sword had fallen, and that these two whom she loved—these two had come to judgment. She did not move ; she only folded her hands and lowered her head to the blow. The thought was revealed in the attitude ; they read it as though she had spoken. There was a quick step forward ; Thurgar was kneeling at her feet ; his upturned face was eloquent with love, and his lips were breathing, tenderly,—

" Mother !"

She started, shot an incredulous glance into his face, then another up into the face of her lover. The smile of a blissful surprise trembled in her eyes a moment, and the next she was lying insensible in the arms of Emory Hild.

CHAPTER XXXI.

It was less than a month later that the good people of Portland awoke to the knowledge that an event had occurred in their midst which did violence to the commonest principles of social courtesy. At the mansion which from lowest stone to topmost tile they had watched with jealous guardianship, which as the repository of municipal pride owed to the body corporate every allegiance,—in that mansion had been privately celebrated a wedding.

It has been from time immemorial the charter-right of a community to canvass for an indefinite time beforehand a contemplated marriage. It is the office of society to herald the dawn of interest; to watch stealthily the premonitions of affection; to compare at different stages the symptoms, and announce if the course be that of normal love, or if it reveals the ominous quality of spasmodic action; and, at last (all explosions and relapses being met and overcome), to set with due ceremonial the seal of matrimony, and—draw a long breath in the conviction of having stood by a duty in that high heroism which exhibits not alone cheerfulness but even enthusiasm. To ignore the prerogative of society is therefore to violate every principle of law and order. And what could be a more aggravated affront than a private marriage in the banker's mansion? What business had Dr. Hild

uniting himself now to Mrs. Rand, when the public had prescribed the proper time years ago? Why on earth should
Mrs. Rand marry at all, when general sentiment had gotten
over requiring it of her? Such an erratic pair! Then the
wedding—that should have set the whole State agog, in a
house that might have accommodated everybody who pre-
tended to be anybody, to dwindle into a petty affair of six—
it was beyond question a civic disgrace.

To the susceptible heart of young ladyhood there was a
double grievance, for it was learned that, after the bridal, had
been celebrated a formal rite of adoption, whereby Arthur
Edgar Wright became Arthur Edgar Hild and legal heir
to the name and estates of both parents. To be defrauded
of this also! Really, the only way the handsome reprobate
could at all atone would be by selecting forthwith a Mrs.
Hild, Jr.; and, who knew? Every one was licensed to hope.

But, as the months advanced, concern for Thurgar's help-
meet began to be overshadowed by interest in rumors,
vague at first and contradictory, of a fortune that had come
into the young man's possession. The practical world is
wary of the exceptional; rare luck is a thing calling for tes-
timony; Portland was not to be committed into surprise,
only to smile later at its credulity. But whispered rumor
had grown soon to material evidence of a system of public
charities instituted in the crowded Eastern centres and
devised upon a scale altogether beyond the warrant of the
banker's wealth. How had the fellow come upon his fortune? Curiosity was at tightest tension. But the won-

der of the people was privileged to meet here a full response; and to-day, in the legends of the town, the tale told first and ever with keenest zest is the story of the insane miner who saved the life of Thurgar Hild and left him the legacy of the mine for which they had tunnelled together. The value of the gift remains a theme of endless conjecture, but the output of ore has brought as yet no hint of exhaustion in the old man's treasury.

The years go by, but the miner's wealth still ministers to good. Over the haunts of want his sorrow hovers in the hand of benediction: and within the protecting piles where the poor and the unfortunate find shelter, many a weary man maimed in body and maimed in soul still breathes a voiceless prayer for poor "daft" Onlucky, who sleeps as he lived amid the kindly solitudes of the Rockies.

In the hearts of the two at last united there is peace,—the deep peace that blossoms out of pain; and over the household broods no shadow, for faith is perfect and love is full: so full that in it is no room for bitterness, and only a saddened pity shades the thought that is wafted to the grave on the heights of the distant Bitter-Root.

THE END.